CMB 36/74

ESSAYS FOR RALPH SHAW

edited by

NORMAN D. STEVENS

The Scarecrow Press, Inc.

Metuchen, N.J.   1975

All royalties earned by this volume are being donated to the Ralph R. Shaw Visiting Scholar Fund (Rutgers)

Library of Congress Cataloging in Publication Data
Main entry under title:

Essays for Ralph Shaw.

Includes index.
CONTENTS: Shaw the person: Martin, L. A tribute to Ralph Shaw. Hines, T. C. Shaw and the machine.--Projects and experiments: Clarke, R. F. Adverse drug reaction information in the literature. Dougherty, R. M. Libraries and innovations. [etc.]
1. Library science--Addresses, essays, lectures.
2. Shaw, Ralph Robert, 1907-1972. I. Shaw, Ralph Robert, 1907-1972. II. Stevens, Norman D.
Z665.E77   020   75-6664
ISBN 0-8108-0815-3

INTRODUCTION

Fancy titles and fancy words often accompany volumes in honor of aging or departed scholars. Such fancy titles and fancy words have no place in a volume of essays for Ralph Shaw, for he was a direct, practical person.

Often such volumes focus on a central theme, seeking to reflect the person's life work and main contribution. Such a focus is not possible in a volume of essays for Ralph Shaw, for he was a person of so many interests. To select one theme would not adequately reflect the multitude of his interests and enthusiasms.

Often such volumes are a series of contributions by the person's contemporaries whether or not they were in any real sense his colleagues. Certainly in the case of Ralph Shaw, he had more contemporaries than colleagues, and even his closest colleagues were often touched by his sharp tongue and sharp pen. It would be difficult to find a suitable group of his contemporaries who could contribute, with appreciation and understanding, essays to a volume in honor of Ralph Shaw.

More appropriate seem to be volumes which reflect the contributions of those who were students of the person being honored. Such is the intent of this volume. While we were not all admirers of Ralph Shaw, we were all, nevertheless, guided and directed by him and strongly felt his influence. He helped shape our thinking about librarianship.

In reviewing the quality of library education in the United States, Chicago in the 1930s and Columbia in the late 1940s are most frequently cited as the instances in which a strong faculty, a good program, and outstanding students combined to bring a lasting distinction to the school and to the profession. To those of us who were at Rutgers in the late 1950s and the early 1960s it seems that those same qualities were present there, although it is perhaps too soon to judge.

iii

Under Lowell Martin's guidance a new graduate program in library service was developed at Rutgers University beginning in 1953. Dean Martin, with strong support from the University, soon brought to Rutgers a truly outstanding faculty which included Paul Dunkin, Mary Gaver, Margaret Monroe, Ralph Shaw, and Richard Shoemaker, among others. A newly developed curriculum, which subsequently influenced curricula elsewhere, emphasized the philosophical aspects of librarianship and provided for a relatively few courses presenting a broad basic training for the profession. The presence of a strong faculty and a strong curriculum attracts strong students. Soon, librarians throughout the country were recommending the Graduate School of Library Service at Rutgers. That is what brought us together.

Shaw replaced Martin as Dean in 1959 and under his leadership plans for the doctoral program were completed and the program was begun in that same year. Just as the master's program had developed rapidly, so did the doctoral program. Shaw sought out good students, found means for providing adequate financial support for them, and relentlessly pushed them to complete the program as quickly as possible. Within two years he had graduated the first students.

The main function of a doctoral program is to teach those in it how to do research and how to present that research. We can each testify that Ralph Shaw, as the driving force behind us, certainly pressed that theme. Despite his many other interests and his frequent absences from the Rutgers campus, he did his best to sharpen our critical abilities.

Almost all of the contributors to this volume were advised by Shaw in the doctoral program at Rutgers. If this volume is to be judged as a whole, it should be in terms of the overall quality of the work presented and not on its relationship to any central theme, real or imagined. It has been from ten to fifteen years since we worked under Shaw. We hope that time plus the training we received under him at Rutgers have helped make us the kind of researchers and writers that he envisaged for that program. To Shaw, and other faculty at Rutgers, we owe a large measure of thanks for the support that they offered and for the skills that they helped us to develop. The weaknesses in our work are the result of our own imperfections and of our inability to live up to what Shaw saw in us.

Norman D. Stevens

iv

CONTENTS

Introduction   iii

I.   SHAW THE PERSON

      A Tribute to Ralph Shaw (Lowell Martin)   3
      Shaw and the Machine (Theodore C. Hines)   6

II.   PROJECTS AND EXPERIMENTS

      Adverse Drug Reaction Information in the
         Literature (Robert F. Clarke)   17
      Libraries and Innovations (Richard M. Dougherty) 23
      Scholars in Residence (Ira W. Harris)   44
      The Real World of Continuing Education for
         Library Personnel (Peter Hiatt)   54
      ESEA Title II Contributions to State Depart-
         ment of Education Leadership of School
         Media Programs (Milbrey L. Jones)   70

III. SCIENTIFIC MANAGEMENT AND STATISTICS

      Compound Growth in Libraries (Fred Heinritz)   88
      Turnover Rate: Basic Library Statistics and
         Some Applications (Theodore S. Huang)   108
      Quali-Quanti as Output Performance Criteria
         (Choong H. Kim)   127
      Inventory (Henry Voos)   140

IV.   THEORY AND PHILOSOPHIES

      Theories of Information (Susan Artandi)   157
      Cooperation Unlimited (Leonard Grundt)   171
      Public and Technical Library Services: A
         Revised Relationship (Doralyn J. Hickey)   179
      Beyond the Promises of Automation (Norman
         D. Stevens)   190

PART I

SHAW THE PERSON

A TRIBUTE TO RALPH SHAW

Lowell Martin

How does one honor a person who was so vividly here and is now gone? In the case of Ralph Shaw the answer is not sad mourning nor sentimental tribute. If this man was nothing else, he was uncompromisingly honest, about himself and with others.

This volume is an entirely suitable tribute. Ralph would have been pleased with it. He would be proud to see the work of his former students, to whom he felt a strong attachment through his gruff exterior. He was a hard worker and would have welcomed this evidence of accomplishment. He was also a hard player, so that--remembering his wry sense of humor--the only other suitable form of tribute I can think of would be an all-night poker game.

I first met Ralph Shaw when as a student at the Graduate Library School of the University of Chicago I was asked to handle temporarily a seminar from which Carleton Joeckel had to be absent for a few weeks. When I went into the class the first day, halfway down the table there was a small, wiry, restless individual. He allowed me to sit down, raised his hand, and asked: "Teacher, can you give me one reason why I should not get my tuition back?"

A few weeks later I went with Ralph to Gary, Indiana, where he was then director of the public library. He was starting bookmobile service out into the county, but in typical Shavian fashion he did not buy several expensive bookmobiles but rather three large truck trailers and one truck cab. No point, he said, in maintaining three motor units when one can move several trailers. So we spent the day racing around in the truck cab, moving first one trailer and then another to new locations to check out the schedule.

3

I remember that, coming back to the main library
that day, Ralph told me with considerable relish how he had
routed traffic in and out of the central building with fool-proof
one-way doors. As we came up to the "In" door the librarian in charge of the main library had somehow managed to
open it from the inside and was coming out the wrong way.
It is one measure of the man that he delighted in telling this
story on himself in later years.

Ralph Shaw went on to the position of Director of the
Department of Agriculture Library in Washington, and during
that period developed the Rapid Selector, the first functioning
automated bibliographical retrieval system. That was in 1946
or 1947. Ten years later he said: "Never use a machine
for that which can be done in half the time and at half the
cost by a human being." Ten years after that he was warning about the limitations of machines in solving human problems. I quickly learned to listen to him if I wanted to anti-
cipate what librarians would be thinking a decade later.

Ralph also started the Scarecrow Press during the
Washington days. Guests at the Shaw home in Georgetown
had after-dinner cognac in the basement, helping Ralph and
Viola pack books to fill the orders that had come in that day.
Years before such presses proliferated, Ralph Shaw developed
a specialized, low-overhead publication house, built it into a
million-dollar enterprise--and paid royalties to every one of
his authors. I always anticipated having someone complain
to Ralph that Scarecrow books left something to be desired
in aesthetic design, because he was at his savage best in
explaining the economics of publishing.

I recall when he visited Rutgers before his appointment to the faculty and he and I talked to the President, Mason
Gross. Dr. Gross called me afterward and said: "We want
that man, but how long will he stay?" Ralph stayed at Rutgers for ten years and they were among the most productive
of his life.

His typical day was 5:00 a.m. to 9:00 a.m. on the
Scarecrow Press--early morning to late afternoon in the classroom and talking to students (he was ingenious in avoiding
committee meetings)--dinner with visitors from the Atomic
Energy Commission or some other government agency with
which he consulted--then in the evening perhaps one of the
many parties that he and Viola gave in their home on River
Road, with guests from across the University.

What do you make of a man who loved to talk over a
bottle of bourbon into the small hours, but who regularly fell
asleep when attending the theater? A man who could not
abide the bureaucracy of the American Library Association
and who served as its president? A teacher who cross-ex-
amined students relentlessly, to the point of tears, and somehow earned their affection in the process? A professor who
produced relatively little research of his own but guided one
of the few sustained series of researches that has occurred
in the library field? The skilled, patient fisherman and the
inept, impulsive automobile driver? The compulsive critic
of all around him, yet a man of absolute personal loyalty?

This was not one man. Professionally he was librarian, educator, administrator, inventor, publisher, government
counselor. Personally he was a mover and shaker, driven
by the conviction that the world was in an unnecessary mess
and that the human brain could solve all problems and human
energy remove all obstacles. He said he judged an individual
by how he walked upstairs--the question was how eager he
was to get to the top and on to doing whatever was to be done
there.

A happy man? Somehow the word does not fit the
restless energy and the caustic wit. To me he was the person I have known who lived most fully, by his lights as to
why we are here. I saw him fight through many a day,
committed and ferocious, and then in the evening, having done
what it was his nature to do, sitting warm and philosophical
over one of Viola's gourmet dinners. Ralph Shaw was a self-
realized man, except that the job was never done.

It is given to few men to make an impress on their
time and place. Ralph Shaw did so, by force of mind, by
force of energy, and by integrity. It is that mark that we
should remember, and not the place that stands empty.

SHAW AND THE MACHINE

Theodore C. Hines

Ralph Shaw was an enthusiastic sharer in the great American romance with technology and equipment. He was an inventor, adapter, adopter, discoverer and tinkerer. Insatiably curious about methods and devices, how things were done, how everything worked, what the principles of operation were, he was also likely to insist on imparting this knowledge to others, sometimes against their resistance to knowing about such non-literary things.

In all this, of course, he was part of a tradition in American librarianship which is too often forgotten. Melvil Dewey, scion of gadget-minded Seventh Day Baptists, was a gadgeteer himself and invented, among other things, the now standard office vertical file. It was John Shaw Billings who gave Herman Hollerith the basic concepts that created IBM. It was the public librarian of Washington, D. C., Dr. George F. Bowerman, who had the idea which Dickman made concrete as the Dickman charging machine--the prototype of today's credit card. Libraries were among the first to accept such newfangled devices as the telephone and the typewriter. Charles Williamson was using marginal punched cards to match Columbia alumni with jobs in the late twenties. It is even alleged that Miss Sanderson of the Columbia Library School invented the red and black typewriter ribbon.

In his brief biography in Who's Who in Librarianship, Shaw mentions only three of his numerous inventions: the rapid selector, the photoclerk and transaction charging.

The rapid selector, which he invented while working with Vannevar Bush, was the first complex piece of equipment designed for searching recorded information. A number of devices in wide use today derive from it. The rapid selector exploited electronics, optics and photography; but the

6

system concept was that of using bibliographic coordination--
coordinate indexing--to locate material rapidly, and to combine this with a means for providing the user with his own
copies of the material in micro or hard copy form. What
was important was the system, not the machine. The machine
was simply an efficient, rapid way to carry out a part of the
system.

The rapid selector, in a version produced by a commercial firm, was in regular use for the Navy Bureau of
Ships while the use of computers for literature searching was
as yet undreamed of. With a clerk at the controls searching
for contract information, it displayed relevant pages of the
documents themselves on its screen, not bibliographic citations. At the push of a button, it would immediately provide
microfilm copies of the appropriate documents for the user,
who could request hard copy in photostat form as well.

Shaw was an early exploiter of the camera for library
purposes. The Department of Agriculture had a network of
far-flung laboratories and experiment stations. To serve
them, Shaw did not resort to interlibrary loan, but rather to
wholesale photostating of journal articles and other documents
which were sent out to the field with a speed of response to
requests which it would be marvelous to be able to find today.

In order that researchers in the field would be helped
rapidly to find out what existed so they could request it, Shaw
used photography and lithography to produce the Bibliography
of Agriculture. It was produced by photographing the original
typed index cards, laid out shingled on page layout boards.
It was a typical Shaw product. It looked like hell, it was
done by a tiny staff, but it often left the printer for the sub-
scriber within five days after the last article indexed had
been received, and it covered a hundred thousand items a
year. The Bibliography of Agriculture in those days neatly
combined current awareness and retrospective searching values before the term for the first had even been thought of.

Again, it was the efficacy of the system which mat-
tered to Shaw, and he used whatever means was most efficient. There are a number of computer-based systems today in which the equipment operates with the speed of summer lightning--but the coverage still manages to be months
behind.

It was the introduction of the idea of copying articles

and giving the copies to the user which led Shaw to become an expert on copyright. It was the use of the photostat to copy articles and the camera to copy shingled index cards which led Shaw to the second of the inventions he listed in his biographical sketch--the photoclerk.

The photoclerk was a sort of miniature photostat machine especially adapted to clerical chores. Shaw designed it and a Department of Agriculture carpenter built the prototype out of scrap plywood. The lens and shutter probably came from a junk shop camera. The thing was designed to use rools of photostat paper, producing a paper negative image.

The photoclerk was operated mechanically by pulling a lever which turned on the lights and tripped the shutter. It was far simpler and, incidentally, far more durable and reliable over its many years of use than the electrically operated Photocharger version commercially produced by Remington Rand.

The prototype had a counter, made by using a standard commercial hand counter rather cleverly tripped by a hinged arm on the operating lever. This provided an automatic record of work performed, and Shaw, of course, was always interested in records of work performed.

It was also supposed to provide a way of knowing when you ran out of paper but it did not work out that way. It was too complicated to keep track of partial rolls and beginning counts.

The indicator and warning system that Shaw dreamed up to deal with this problem was ingenious, as many of Shaw's devices were. Ingredients: one piece of coat hanger wire bent in a 'U' shape, one screw, two screw eyes and the bell from an old mechanical alarm clock.

The bottom of the coat hanger 'U' passed through the two screw eyes. These were fastened at the top back of the inside of the photoclerk to form a hinge so that the arms of the 'U' swung freely up and down. One arm of the 'U', its end bent in a curl to add weight and to make it slide smoothly, rested on top of the roll of photographic paper. The other stuck through a light-trapped hole to the outside of the box. As the paper was used, the arm resting on it fell lower. So too, of course, did the outside arm, which moved against a scale showing how much paper was left.

When the roll ran out, the inside arm could drop past
the roll core to hit the alarm clock bell, which was screwed
to the inside of the box at the point where the weighted end
of the arm would hit. Mechanically simple, highly reliable,
cheap, efficient and clever--typically Shaw.

As a device, the photoclerk disappeared when xerog-
raphy became cheap and readily available. As a system concept of using cheap mechanical copying rather than typing
repetitive information, it is not adequately exploited by most
libraries even today.

The third invention listed by Shaw was transaction
charging. In its original form, it used a photoclerk to record loan information in transaction order and the first commercial version was, as noted earlier the Remington Rand
photocharger.

It is often said that Shaw "invented photocharging" but
note that he himself did not phrase it in that way. What he
invented was a system, not a gadget--it was transaction
charging, and the system could be (and has been) carried
out manually, with cameras of various kinds, with audio
recording equipment, and with computers. Transaction
charging was the first conceptual advance in charging systems since just after the turn of the century. Widely used
as it is, it still remains to be as fully exploited as it usefully can be, and is still little understood, even by some of
its users.

It was typical of Shaw to see that what he had was a
system and not a device. He taught about library circulation
system in that way, too. His course lectures were organized from the point of view of the few underlying concepts
rather than around the broad variety of equipment used to
implement them. It was not only an approach which made
the variety easier to learn, it was also one which was far
more meaningful.

Exploiting photography as a systems aid was something which occupied Shaw off and on for many years. Some
thought that offset from typescript made the books he published at the Scarecrow Press hideous, but he produced books
others would not accept without subsidy because the market
for them was too limited, he always paid royalties, and he
always made money on them. Cuss Scarecrow as much as
you like, but try to imagine your professional and reference
collections without the Scarecrow Press books. I know, too,

that Shaw did not do what I once saw a university press do
when confronted with an excellent index to an important book
--cut it in half because the editor felt that setting the index
in smaller type than the text would make the book "aesthe-
tically displeasing." Poor typography and careless proof-
reading are visible to the user, but the kind of intellectual
shoddiness represented in the university press incident unfortunately is not.

To Shaw, there was nothing to admire in the cataloger
or bibliographer who believed in cataloging or bibliography as
a necromantic art performed for the aesthetic satisfaction of
the practitioner. The point, and the only point, of cataloging,
indexing, and bibliographic work is to provide the cheapest
and best user access to materials as quickly as possible.

It was the combination of this philosophy with Shaw's
perception that the use of photography made copying quick,
cheap and something which could be delegated which made
the Shaw-Shoemaker bibliographies possible. Photography
reduced copying errors, too, which made the Shaw-Shoemaker
lists not only more comprehensive but more accurate in some
respects than Evans or Sabin or Roorbach and Kelly. Shoemaker, a great scholar and a great man, wanted to look at
books, to verify. Shaw said no; it was better to have an
imperfect listing than one which was never finished. So,
despite the views of aesthetic bibliographers and the Bibliographic Society of America, a gap in the U. S. national bibliography was filled by a system, photography, and determination.

Miniprint was another idea of Shaw's, again exploiting
photography, and again before its time. The concept was to
use an opaque, paper rather than transparent film, like
Microcard, in an edition printing process, like Microprint,
but using a reduction ratio which would produce or document
readable (or consultable, in the case of reference tools) with
the naked eye or, at most, with the aid of a simple lens.
NATO issued documents in miniprint, and Shaw published
some of his students' dissertations in this way as a demonstration, but the system was not really taken up. Considering, however, the two-volume version of the Oxford English
Dictionary which was fairly recently published in a similar
format, I would not want to say that Shaw's idea was not
sound. Scarecrow also continues to produce large reference
works in Miniprint, although in a type size which no longer
requires any reading aid.

Shaw's interest in equipment, machines, and devices
was not at all limited to photographic applications, nor even
to serious things. I gave him a toy once which, I believe,
gave him considerable pleasure. At any rate, he kept it on
his desk, bought it new batteries, and watched visitors push
its switch with pleased anticipation until it broke. The device was very simple: a black box with a switch. When the
switch was turned on, the box whirred, a door opened, and
a rather gruesome plastic hand came out, turned the switch
off, went back in the box and shut the door behind it. Finis.
Rather like some library computer applications, wasn't it?

Shaw liked big, complex automobiles, filled with gad-
getry, that lay flat on the road, and he drove them at high
speeds. He liked household gadgets of all kinds, from dish-
washers to patent corkscrews to soda-makers, and tended to
acquire them, display them, and forget them.

I remember a typical situation involving equipment
which illustrates both Shaw's kindness and his brutality.
There was a lady in the library who was an immensely
skilled reference librarian who was growing slowly deaf.
Her deafness interfered with her work. She tried to con-
ceal it, and in so doing turned from a warm and friendly
person to someone apparently cold, aloof, and condescending.
Her subordinates did not dare speak to her about it but did
bring the matter to Shaw's attention. He suggested that she
see a doctor about a hearing aid. He spoke reassuringly
about hearing aids being like eyeglasses, something one had
to resort to.

Nothing worked. The lady had the illogical but too
common feeling that to admit to deafness was to confess
something sinful. She drove complex cars and used complex cameras, but felt that rapid selectors and photoclerks
and hearing aids were technical, and hence beyond her.
Shaw was technical, too, and to her mind interested in output rather than quality, and hence beyond the pale.

Finally, Shaw called her in and informed her that unless she either got a hearing aid or a statement from her
physician that her case would not be helped by one, he would
begin proceedings for her dismissal.

On the following Monday, she came into the office
wearing a hearing aid. There was a period of adjustment,
of course, but in a short time she was her old self again.

She never forgave Shaw, though, and I wonder whether she ever saw what he had done for her. When I told her I was leaving my Washington job to go back to library school to work on a doctorate, she said how nice, and then asked me where I was going. "Rutgers," I told her.

"You don't want to go there," she said, "Shaw's there. He hates people. He only likes machines."

Shaw constantly, no matter what else he was doing, played with ideas for equipment. I remember, in the earliest days of optical character recognition, watching him drawing matrices and filling them with little blackened squares during a faculty meeting. He was, at the same time, participating vigorously and a little dictatorially in the discussion. I asked afterwards, and found out that he was trying to find out how small a matrix was adequate to represent the alphabet and numbers unambiguously.

In view of all this, his attitude toward computers often seemed curious to outsiders, who regarded him as a kind of Luddite. To those who worked closely with him there was neither inconsistency nor any anti-machine sentiment involved. After all, he had encouraged his students to learn to program. He had enthusiastically endorsed Dr. Susan Artandi's early experimental work on automatic indexing by computer, securing support for her work through the Air Force Office of Scientific Research, under Dr. Harold Wooster, just as he secured support for most of the doctoral students at Rutgers. Later, he brought experts in computer applications to the University of Hawaii.

Shaw's denunciations of computer applications were just that--denunciations of applications, not of equipment. At one stage he remarked, in that aggressive, challenging manner of his, that he had yet to see a computer application in librarianship or information handling which could not be carried out better, faster, and cheaper by manual means. This remark enraged a small but significant section of the information community, one which already felt beleaguered in its efforts to persuade librarians that they could not afford not to embrace the new technology.

In retrospect, as usual, there was right on both sides. Shaw was probably quite correct in his assessment that, at that time, good manual methods were better, often by far, than existing computer applications. The computer innovators, whether in order to better justify their need for massive infusions of grant money or for other reasons, were likely to give the impression of massive accomplishment when what was really going on was necessarily massive experimentation. It was this misrepresentation, the statements in which projected goals read as if they were economic working systems, which most annoyed Shaw.

Shaw often rather approvingly quoted someone's story about the analysis of a system for the purpose of computerizing it which resulted in such a massive clean-up of bad procedures in the old system that the computer was found to be unnecessary. He was suspicious of my feeling, and that of others, that it was often necessary to bring in the new equipment as a means of prodding the recalcitrant even to look at the old system. Indeed, Shaw felt that in some instances a computer was used to execute part of an operation as an excuse to avoid examining the system as a whole.

Although he was an early, vigorous exponent of the application of the principles of scientific management and operations research to library problems, and although he required a course in statistics of all his doctoral candidates, Shaw had a healthy suspicion of over-complex analysis of library problems.

It was his basic belief that the level of management performance in library and information work was so low that if relatively gross analysis did not reveal how major service improvements and savings could be made, you had tackled the wrong problem area. Consequently, he felt that there was little necessity for sophisticated analytical techniques.

Underlying much of Shaw's use of equipment was the basic tenet that labor was expensive and that material, properly used, was cheap. He was fairly constantly enraged, too, at the habit librarians had of considering the purchase of equipment a current, rather than a capital, expenditure, maintaining, I think justly, that this primitive viewpoint was a major contributor to library mismanagement.

His interest in information service was, of course, ecumenical. In his career, he was a public librarian, special librarian, information scientist, university librarian, publisher, and library educator. He literally could not see the distinctions the divisionists among us wish to perpetrate between serving the disadvantaged, the scientist, the

housewife. All were entitled to the best service we could
provide. Nor did he fall for those "management studies"
which indicated that we could effect savings by shoving our
work off on the user--as if the user's time were worth
nothing. Contrary, too, to some current trends, he saw
nothing "servile" in the concept of service. He was as concerned about bookmobile service to the "disadvantaged" and
to children as about service to the engineer and scientist--
after all, it was he who invented the idea of using the trac-
tor trailer as a bookmobile so as to provide more service
at less cost. Despite the fact that false humanists, and
even some real humanists, never believed it, he felt strongly
that the same kinds of resources mobilized to serve science
and engineering, especially in the immediate post-Sputnik
era, should be mobilized to serve the humanities.

Shaw was never silly enough to believe that librarianship was a science; it was a service profession. Nor did
he think that documentation yet deserved the name of information science. It could get there, with hard work, with
development from an empirical base; but it would not become more scientific by theorizing in the absence of, or in
ignorance of, data.

Further, and more to the point, he never tired of
saying that the machine is not the system. Advances do not
come out of the employment of the machine, however wisely
it may be employed. Rather, they spring from conceptualiza-
tion of ways to meet needs.

Shaw would ask hard questions. He might ask, for
example, very pointed ones about many of our computerized,
automated libraries. Do they produce more and better access to materials per employee today than they did in 1930?
Do materials get in the catalogs and on the shelves faster?
Do we provide significant new services to our users?

Shaw did not, certainly, say it couldn't be done. Nor
did he say it shouldn't be done using the machine--computer,
camera, or whatever was the best way to do it. What he
did say was that it mostly wasn't being done, and there was
no point in using equipment to hide the fact. He would have
agreed with the idea that, of course, more research, more
theory, more knowledge are needed by information science,
but the advantage to the user would be enormous if we simply applied what we already know.

PART II

PROJECTS AND EXPERIMENTS

ADVERSE DRUG REACTION INFORMATION
IN THE LITERATURE

Robert F. Clarke

The purpose of the survey on which this essay is
based was to learn the opinions among health professionals
about adverse drug reaction information (ADRI) available
today.

A questionnaire was sent by the Food and Drug Administration (FDA) to more than 1,700 health care professionals, primarily physicians (internists and family practice
specialists) and pharmacists (members of the American Society of Hospital Pharmacists), but also to others, including
instructors, researchers, drug information centers, medical
libraries, etc. The survey asked questions about their ADRI
communication patterns and their opinions about ADRI, and
76.4 per cent of the questionnaires returned were usable.
What follows is a tabulation and analysis of the responses.

Importance of Adverse Drug Reaction Information

Table I shows that 65 per cent of those questioned
felt that ADRI was "very" or "extremely" important to them.
This percentage would be even higher if only respondents'
replies were included in the table. In order not to bias the
figure, the 407 persons who did not return the questionnaire
were counted in the "not at all" category. Thus, it is clear
that the health professionals surveyed are definitely interested in ADRI.

Use of Adverse Drug Reaction Information

Table II shows data sought on the purpose to which

17

TABLE I

The Importance of Information on Adverse
Reactions to Questionnaire Recipients

Importance	Number	Percent
Extremely Important	623	36.1
Very Important	498	28.9
Somewhat Important	160	9.3
Not At All Important	443[a]	25.7
Totals	1,724	100.0%

[a]Including 407 questionnaire recipients who did not respond.

TABLE II

Professional Identification of Respondent
Related to the Purposes for Which
Information Is Used, in Percents

Purpose	Identification	
	Prac. pharm.	Prac. phys.
To advise health practitioners	87	34
To detect adverse reactions	63	73
To advise, treat patients	52	90
To teach the health sciences	27	36
others, d.k., n.a.	7	6
Total N[a]	(599)	(284)

[a]Total N = 883, excluding the 31%, or 398, with professional identification of other than practicing pharmacist or physician.

ADRI was put by the respondents. These data are based on returns only from practicing physicians and practicing pharmacists. Reasons other than the main four have been collected under the category, "Others, d. k. (don't know), n. a. (not applicable)." This latter category, though, is so low (6-7 per cent) that it is not meaningful in comparison with the other categories. Clearly, the pharmacist's need for ADRI is related to, but different from, that of the physician. While 87 per cent of the practicing pharmacists use ADRI to "advise health practitioners," in contrast, 90 per cent of practicing physicians use it for "advising and treating patients." This finding should surprise no one. Of more importance is the finding that both groups secondarily share an interest in "detecting adverse reactions." The implication of this is that both groups seek signs of reactions that could lead to medication changes and perhaps to the reporting of adverse reactions.

Major Sources of Adverse Drug Reaction Information

Table III lists the major sources of ADRI as indicated by respondents. Clearly, multiple sources are used. Two pharmaceutical manufacturer-sponsored sources closely follow the leader. It is notable that the limited circulation

TABLE III

Major Sources of Information on
Adverse Drug Reactions, in Percents

Source

Medical Letter	50. 0
Manufacturer's Literature	47. 5
Physicians Desk Reference	46. 1
Clinical Experience Abstracts	35. 8
Journal of the American Medical Assoc.	34. 3
Amer. Hosp. Formulary Serv.	32. 6
Clin-Alert	32. 4
Drug Intell. and Clin. Pharm.	30. 5
Total N	(1, 281)
Mean answers per respondent	4. 35

(2,000 plus) publication of the Food and Drug Administration's
Clinical Experience Abstracts ranks fourth. It should also
be noted that the FDA approves the information appearing in
the Physicians Desk Reference, and the FDA has regulatory
authority over manufacturers' advertising. While the FDA
chooses what information appears in Clinical Experience
Abstracts, it does not originate the information itself on adverse reactions, but relies on articles appearing in the recognized professional journals. Thus, pharmaceutical manufacturers and the FDA play a leading role in ADRI consulted
by those surveyed. Professional sources, as found through
JAMA (Journal of the American Medical Association) and the
American Hospital Formulary Service (AHFS) fall further
down the scale.

Ease of Locating Adverse Drug Reaction Information

        Table IV indicates that respondents felt that it is
neither "very easy" nor "very difficult" to locate needed
ADRI. The sources in the open literature which are available to those that seek ADRI can be used, but ADRI is not
as easy to obtain as it might be.

        Looking more closely at this, Table V shows that
there are many reasons for this difficulty. Not surprisingly,
"poor information on frequency of occurrence" leads the
reasons. Obviously, this is a problem for the reporter who
is writing in the literature about adverse reactions. The
reporter likely will have only limited knowledge through isolated cases, unless a research project is reported which
covers a large-scale experiment, or unless the reporter has
tracked down and united isolated cases.

        A comparison of the negative reasons in Table V
shows that cumulatively, dissatisfaction with quality or content is greater than dissatisfaction with style or format, if
the percentages of the two groups are added. However,
there is sufficient dissatisfaction with style and format to
warrant improvement and the latter are easier to improve
upon than quality or content.

Conclusions

        The survey indicates that health care professionals
feel that ADRI is important to them. It shows that

TABLE IV

The Overall Ease of Locating Needed Information
on Adverse Drug Reactions, in Percents

Perceived Ease	Frequency Distribution
Very easy	16. 6
Somewhat easy	39. 7
Somewhat difficult	38. 2
Very difficult	3. 6
d. k. , n. a.	1. 9
Total N	(1, 281)

TABLE V

Negative Reasons for the Rating Given the Overall Ease
of Locating Needed Information on Adverse
Drug Reactions, in Percents

Reason	Frequency Distribution
Poor information on frequency of occurrence	33. 6
Poor information on clinical significance	31. 3
Lack of cumulative index	25. 4
Poor indexing of adverse reactions	25. 1
Poor information on long-term effects	25. 0
Poor information on size of toxic doses	22. 4
Information not timely	15. 5
Poor format, organization	12. 9
Poor library, reference sources available	10. 5
None, d. k. , n. a.	35. 5
Total N	(1, 281)
Mean answers per respondent	2. 37

pharmacists use ADRI to advise others, while physicians use it primarily to advise and treat patients, and that, secondarily, both groups of practicing professionals use it in detecting adverse reactions. Further, the survey reveals that many sources are used for gathering ADRI. Pharmaceutical industry sources rank number two and number three on the list of most used multiple sources, and a limited distribution source from FDA, Clinical Experience Abstracts, based on articles in the biomedical journal literature, ranks fourth. Those surveyed felt it was both not difficult and not easy to locate ADRI; and that, mostly, quality or content of ADRI could be improved, but that style and format could be also improved.

LIBRARIES AND INNOVATIONS*

Richard M. Dougherty

Academic libraries face a troubled, uncertain future. The recent abrupt leveling of library funding signaled the end of the period of affluence libraries enjoyed throughout the last decade. Moreover, the current budgetary problems have prompted many university officials and legislators to scrutinize library budgets. They want to know if the current costs of libraries are justified, and whether the quality of an institution's program would be impaired if book acquisition rates and library services were reduced. Librarians, too, have begun to reexamine the objectives of their organizations. Are the traditional objectives still appropriate?

Although changes in the budgetary climate represent the most pressing library concern, the budget by no means constitutes the only problem facing today's library manager. New patterns in teaching and research; breakdowns in library operating procedures; and growing library staff discontent all have contributed to today's vexing, difficult questions. Recent events have prompted several distinguished library managers to step down prematurely from their positions.[1] The restiveness of library staffs is frequently cited as the major cause for this recent turnover. Although it constitutes one contributant, as is reflected by the recent development of the ARL Management Review and Analysis Program, the causes are much more complex.[2]

In general, the ability of academic librarians to serve their constituencies has declined steadily over the last few years, but vocal user dissatisfaction only recently began to surface.

---

*A survey made possible by a Council on Library Resources Fellowship.

Although libraries and their management are under
attack from many quarters, librarians have not been oblivious
to the changes occurring about them.[3] Library developments
in automation, networks, national and regional lending libraries, shared cataloging, centralized processing, academic
consortia and the MRAP program, cited previously, all attest to the willingness and ability of library managers to consider and apply new solutions to old problems.

The purpose of this investigation was to identify innovative solutions to existing library organizational, bibliographical, and service problems.[4] The investigator attempted
to identify what librarians were doing which they considered
innovative. The task was to identify the purpose of the innovation; how the innovation had been funded; how permanent funding would be secured (assuming that the innovative
project proved effective); what problems the project had encountered and what solutions had been developed; and most
importantly, what changes in the library's organization,
staffing patterns, and service posture the innovative project
might produce in the foreseeable future.[5]

A Profile of Library Innovations

The projects reviewed were quite varied, but the
majority could be classified into one of four broad categories:[6]

1. Automation of specific library operations, such
    as book ordering, accounting, serials check-in,
    and circulation systems.

2. Computerized bibliographical information sys-
    tems.[7,8,9] The systems at Lehigh University,
    the University of Georgia and UCLA are illus-
    trative projects. Users are provided with bib-
    liographic citations generated from machine read-
    able data bases such as Chem Condensates, ERIC,
    and Biological Abstracts. The products of these
    systems may be used as the basis for either SDI
    services, retrospective literature searches, or
    both.[10]

3. Discipline-oriented information systems. These
    systems are intended to serve well-defined groups
    of specialists. The systems are distinguished

from the projects cited in category two in that
the data are collected, organized, coded, and input locally and the data are not generally available to other centers. Also, the subject content
of the data bases is usually much more specialized than the commercially produced data bases.
The International Treaty Information System, located at the University of Washington, Seattle,
and the Arid Lands Information System, at the
University of Arizona, were two systems serving
specialists. [11],[12]

4. Design of new library services. These projects
usually focused on the current information needs
and information gathering habits of students, faculty and/or researchers. The data once collected
are used to assist planners who intend to design
and develop programs of library services. The
Students' Chemical Information Project, funded by
the Office of Scientific and Technical Information
in Great Britain, represented one significant attempt to provide tailored information services to
academic researchers;[13] whereas the projects observed in the libraries at Hamline University,
St. Paul, Minnesota, and Bath Institute of Technology, Bath, England, were efforts to improve
services to students. [14],[15]

Description of Selected Projects

Automation. --The availability of MARC data has stimulated automation activities in many libraries. Today, the
use of MARC data is almost commonplace, but in 1971 the
situation was markedly different. Most projects were either
in the talking or planning stages. Few systems were as advanced as those observed at the libraries of Georgia Tech
and Trinity College, Dublin, Ireland. These libraries had
designed comprehensive processing sub-systems utilizing
MARC data.

At Georgia Tech the automated processing system began with the selection process. Book selectors were provided with classified subject lists printed from MARC data.
The printouts could be characterized as a specialized SDI
system. The machine-readable data of titles selected for
purchase were used later to generate order forms, catalog
card sets and other pertinent processing control records.

The Trinity College Library processed MARC records produced by the British National Bibliography. Operational automated acquisition, cataloging and processing sub-systems were already in evidence. Moreover, the library had already begun to plan and develop a book catalog based on data in machine-readable form.

One obvious limitation of MARC-based processing systems is the scope of the MARC data base itself. One reason why the Trinity College project had proved so effective was that a large proportion of its acquisitions were represented by British depository items, which were the books upon which the BNB MARC data were based. Georgia Tech, too, reported that a sizeable percentage of its acquisitions were covered by MARC data.

Larger institutions have found that MARC data encompasses only about half of their acquisitions. Consequently, larger libraries must operate parallel technical processing operations. The need to extend the coverage of MARC data has long been recognized. Although MARC coverage was expanded recently to include current French language materials, further expansions merit a high priority. The overall efficiency of computerized processing systems is in part dependent upon the availability of centrally produced machine-readable records.

Circulation systems were commonly observed examples of successful automation projects. The on-line circulation system developed by the library at Ohio State University was a particularly notable accomplishment. Selected data from the main shelf list catalog has been converted into machine-readable form. Readers may access the data base by means of CRT or typewriter terminals. Books may be charged out, reserved, and renewed without physically approaching the circulation desk.[16] The system represents an important breakthrough in library service because it frees the user from the need to consult the card catalog.

The "mini"-catalog experiment at Bath University represented a different approach to the handling and displaying of bibliographical records. The primary objective was to produce a catalog which would be used principally as a finding list. A typical entry included the following data elements: language, shelf location, date of publication, publication format, author, title, and SBN. Similar bibliographic principles to those exemplified by the Bath "mini" catalog project were

presented recently by MacDonald and Elrod.[17] The mini-
catalog concept could harbinger a new era in library catalog
development and lead ultimately to far-reaching changes in
library bibliographic apparatus.

Some libraries have begun to develop specialized bibliographic tools. This has been made possible because data
in machine-readable form are much more easily manipulated
than printed records. The Library of the University of New-
castle-upon-Tyne has developed a software package to produce
specialized catalogs. The generalized software enables them
to print bibliographies listing materials which are quite different in format--for example, technical reports, rare books,
and manuscripts.

Computerized information/bibliographic systems. --
There is no need to detail here the kinds of services that
computerized systems provide. This has already been reported extensively in the literature. Although the systems
already cited, i. e. , UCLA, Georgia, and Ohio State, are
similar in many respects, each institution has approached
the problems of systems development, project management,
and product marketing differently. For example, the Ohio
State Library used off-the-shelf software packages as the
basis of its system, whereas Georgia and UCLA decided to
incur the greater costs of developing more specialized but
flexible software packages locally. There are now many difficult managerial problems associated with the operation of
these systems, but some of them had only begun to loom on
the horizon in 1971. Now, questions such as financing and
marketing have become priority concerns of system managers.
Some of these problems are discussed later in this essay.

The provision of information generated from computer
systems has improved user access to bibliographic data, but
this improved access to data has exposed further the inability
of most libraries to retrieve and deliver physical documents
fast enough in the opinion of many users. The problem is
not an easy one to ameliorate because large academic libraries are complicated to use, and many users are not
skilled in the art of locating library materials. In an effort
to improve document delivery effectiveness, a few libraries
have introduced systems which move library materials directly to requestors.[18] Document delivery systems are now
in operation at Ohio State University, Georgia Tech, and the
University of California, Berkeley. Initial user reactions to
these services seem to be quite favorable.

In the long run the combination of computerized information systems, on-line circulation/inventory systems which
display data on CRTs, document delivery systems, and regional service libraries, as exemplified by the National Lending Library, Boston Spa, England, could affect the fundamental organization of academic libraries. When data are
displayed to a user in his/her office, and documents are
delivered physically to his/her place of work, the need for
some users to go to the library is diminished. These new
systems and services may create different library use patterns which in turn could ultimately alter the shape of library buildings.

Discipline-oriented information systems. --Discipline-
oriented informations systems were not initially considered
within the scope of the survey. These systems are usually
administered independently of the library and, therefore, are
not viewed as a "library" system. But visits to three campuses caused the author to alter this point of view. The
systems observed were the International Treaty Information
System, University of Washington; the Poison Control System, University of British Columbia; and Tree Ring Research Center and the Arid Lands Information Systems, both
located at the University of Arizona. Each system processes
information, and each system is designed to serve the information needs of a specialized group of users. Although each
system designer had achieved a certain measure of success
in producing data in formats specially suited to the needs of
a targeted user group, each system also seemed to lack
sophistication. All were obviously inflexible, cumbersome
and overly expensive. For example, each system was designed either around fixed fields or an eighty-column tab
card or both. Most library system designers have long been
conscious of the limitations of these two design parameters,
but these constraints might not be so obvious to a dendrolo-
gist, a geographer, or a political scientist who develops his
own home-made system. He may not understand the com-
plexities of processing information until after it is too late.
At one installation the researchers had only recently recognized that they had developed a dead-end system which no
longer satisfied the project's information requirements.
Their only recourse was to scrap the system and to start
over. Had they sought expert advice? Yes, from the computer center. Unfortunately, they still had not comprehended
that data handling produces problems distinct from other administrative needs. In this particular case, the researchers
relied upon the advice of an administrative programmer

whose experience had been limited to accounting and payroll
systems. The programmer was in the process of designing
a new, fixed-field system, although it was clear that one requirement of the system was the need to process variable
length records.

Why hadn't these researchers consulted a librarian?
There were librarians on each campus who possessed special
systems expertise. The answers are not obvious, but two
possible explanations were cited. First, the designers never
considered the possibility that the library could help them;
and second, the designer wanted to stay free of the established library bureaucracy.

There seems to be little question but that the designers
could have profited from the advice of others. Librarians
could have served as consultants without involving themselves
in the administration of the system. If librarians don't lend
their assistance to such groups, it is almost certain that
another specialist group will emerge to fill the vacuum.

New library services. --All of the projects observed
were aimed at up-grading the quality of information services.
The major differences were in the approaches taken by the
project managers. In some cases the major thrust of the
project was to forge a stronger link between a computerized
information system and its users. In others, the project
thrust was to identify the needs of users first and then to design services which more closely matched those of a targeted
user group. The Information Officer Program, funded by
OSTI, is a program which is attempting to diffuse computerized bibliographic services throughout selected scientific
groups in order to affect the information use patterns of
these groups.[19]

In contrast, the Information Officer program operated
by the Hamline University Library reflects a concerted effort to focus library services on the classroom needs of faculty and students. The information officers work with students and faculty in the classroom as well as in the library.
The library information officers may provide students with
specialized reading lists, tabulations of data, copies of journal articles and, in one case, with a classroom examination.[20] These information services seemed to be well received by students and faculty. But several critical questions
remain to be answered. Is the personal approach economic-
ally viable? Can a handful of professional librarians serve

a campus of thousands? Could success actually signal ulti-
mate failure by generating user demands which cannot be
met? As these new services become known to more users,
there is a distinct possibility that demands could exceed system resources.

System Performance and Evaluation

Most systems observed were too new to have under-
gone a thorough evaluation. Some project officers had not
yet defined "success" or how to measure it. To some, success was defined as a project which survived the transition
from an experimental status to an operational status. To
others, success was to be measured in terms of cost effectiveness. Still others felt that success should be related to
the degree to which the system altered established information gathering behavior of users and/or their attitudes toward
the library.

The evaluation techniques cited can be summarized as
follows:

1. Precision/recall measures. Measure whether or
    not the citations generated by a system were rele-
    vant to a researcher's information needs.

2. Machine performance of the system. Measure
    the amount of time and effort required of the
    user to access the information he desires. The
    system monitors each search and maintains a
    permanent record of search strategy and results.

3. Willingness to pay. Will users pay for value re-
    ceived? If after a trial period of free searches,
    a user is willing to pay for services received,
    the system is judged to be successful.

4. System economics. Measure and compare unit
    costs against those of a predecessor system.

5. Changes in user behavioral patterns. Measure
    library use patterns of researchers who received
    services to determine if the system generated
    new or different demands for materials.

Overall, system designers had not assigned a high

priority to evaluation at the time of the visits. The upper-
most priority was getting the system into operation. From
a researcher's point of view, the absence of identifiable
evaluation criteria could be viewed as a project plan weakness, but very few library innovative projects were actually
found to be research efforts. Most would be better characterized as developmental projects. Nevertheless, library
managers would be wise to demonstrate how new systems
contribute to the objectives of the parent institution. It is
unlikely that academic administrators and/or legislators will
be willing to authorize permanent funding for an innovative
project without objective evidence of the system's utility and
effectiveness.

Obstacles to Library Innovations

Library innovators have encountered a variety of problems. The problems identified in this survey included non-
receptive library staffs, archaic and inflexible library organizations, apathetic users, inadequate funding, poor planning,
and ineffective implementation. A review of the most frequently cited problems may provide some useful guidance to
other developers.

Resistance of library staffs.--A library staff may not
be prepared to function in the working environment created
by the new system. Some staff members might not even be
aware of the innovative project, and more importantly they
might not understand how the project could affect their personal career status. Is it any wonder that staff might re-
sist a new project, if they believed their jobs would be
placed in jeopardy by the innovation?

A library's administration should work closely with
the staff from the inception of an innovative project, through
its development to its final implementation. Although computerized information systems will undoubtedly produce
changes in the careers of some professionals and non-pro-
fessionals, the threat to job security and status perceived
by some staff is largely unwarranted. Their uneasiness can
be traced, in part, to a lack of information.

Structure of library organizations.--Today's academic
libraries are hierarchical organizations and usually follow
the organizational model of a division into two parts--tech-
nical services and public services. Activities which

transcend the established lines of authority tend to confound traditional lines of communication, and eventually produce interpersonal frictions and conflicts. Innovative projects by definition are new, and therefore may not be part of regular operating procedures.

A library's administration should decide as early as possible where a new activity will eventually fit into the established library organizational structure. The problems of introducing new services into hierarchical organizations should not be underestimated.

Apathetic users. --Library users often appear to be apathetic toward innovative activities. These reactions can sometimes be traced to frustrations they had experienced with libraries previously. These frustrations may have motivated the user to develop a personal information system rather than to depend on the library to satisfy his needs. [21,22] In other words, the user no longer relies on or needs the library to supply him with materials or information. User apathy could also reflect the fact that some researchers don't use information from published literature.

Apparent user disinterest can sometimes be traced to ineffective or nonexistent marketing efforts. Some library developers have paid lip-service only to the question of marketing. Rogers reports that marketing is one key step in the process of diffusing new ideas and products. [23] In order to interest users in a new service, the library must be able to convince users that the new service is worthwhile, and must demonstrate also that the new service is better than the one it is replacing. Marketing is no less important than the creative development effort itself.

Library users themselves occasionally misuse the services of new systems, as they too are conditioned to a traditional behavior pattern. At one institution, users were known to cut out and paste citations from computer listings onto 3 x 5 cards.

Timeliness of services also affects user behavior. If the appearance of a computer-produced bibliography does not coincide with a user's need for the information, the printout will likely be set aside. Obviously, the old library adage of "the right book, at the right place, at the right time" still applies. One developer attempted to improve the timeliness of his monthly SDI printouts by cumulating the

citations into a personal data bank which could be consulted
at the time the need for information occurred.   Obviously,
user education programs should be viewed as another integral
step in the innovation process.

Project funding. --Projects have been funded from several different sources.   These include: 1) governmental
agencies, 2) private foundations, 3) local institutions, 4) user
charges, and 5) combinations of governmental or local budgets and user charges.   Federal agencies have served as
the principle source for seed money.   However, several directors reported that they were beginning to charge users
for services rendered.

Projects funded exclusively with outside funds reach a
crisis point when the outside funding is terminated and the
organization must make the transition to local funding.   The
risk of failure seems to be greatest at this point.   Projects
funded from local funds don't have to grapple with this problem.   Their principal problem seems to be in securing the
initial capital to fund the project.

Most library administrators interviewed recognized
the need to develop local sources of funding.   Some believed
that a cost recovery mechanism based on user charges held
promise as a viable solution.   This opinion was held in spite
of the fact that the user charge schemes in actual operation
seemed to recover only a small portion, usually as little as
5 to 15 per cent, of the total operating costs.

Most library administrators sought permanent funds
in the form of regular budget augmentations.   Since the funding prospects for higher education are so bleak, one wonders
whether the future of important new projects should be left
to such uncertainties.   It is indeed paradoxical that at a time
when more librarians seemed willing to adopt innovative approaches to problem solving, money became tight.

As funds become tighter, the willingness of an organization to take innovative risks declines because slack resources disappear.   An organization can ill afford to make
mistakes when funds are scarce.   In other words, the budgetary risks associated with innovations are increased.

A few of the project directors and administrators
interviewed seemed unwilling to face the current budgetary
climate realistically.   They are willing to gamble the long-

term success of their projects on a blind faith that the additional funds will somehow become available, if for no other
reason than because "their project was deserving"--a risky
strategy.

If libraries are to adopt new service patterns at a
time when funding is static, they must be willing to review
and reassess current library objectives and service priorities.
If a non-traditional service is deemed sufficiently important
in relation to traditional services, then funding commitments
to existing services may have to be reduced in order to generate stable funding for the new activity. If innovative activities are sacrificed in order to preserve existing activities,
librarians will eventually force their organizations into operational straitjackets.

One strategy a library might apply, in an effort to re-
lease existing dollar resources, is to initiate thorough programs of procedural analysis and work simplification. Most
large libraries seriously under-utilize their staff resources.
Professional staff engage in activities which are either totally unnecessary or could be performed better by support
staff. The potential savings generated through work simplification in some libraries might actually exceed 20 per cent
of the personnel budget. One paper published recently by
William Axford demonstrates what might be achieved through
work simplification studies. [24]

The funding policies of some federal agencies have
also proved, on occasion, to be counter-productive to innovation. There seems to be a tendency to underfund projects,
or to fund them for too short a period of time. Some funding agencies expect too much too soon. When one considers
the number of years it has taken projects such as the Ohio
College Library Center, the Stanford BALLOTS Project, the
Computer Information Systems at the University of California
at Los Angeles and the University of Georgia to achieve
operational status, it becomes clear that considerable time
and money are required to develop and implement large
scale, nontraditional information systems. Although funders
themselves have to work under special constraints (they too
have to demonstrate the cost-effectiveness of their projects
to superiors), it would be wise if funders adopted a more
realistic framework for financing library projects.

Every effort should be made by funding agencies to
insure that a project is provided with adequate funding

throughout the duration of the project. At the same time,
funding agencies should require each library that receives
developmental funds to cultivate local sources of funding.
A system of phased cost-sharing represents one plausible
approach. Funding of large-scale projects could be spread
out over several years, with the grantee institution assuming
a larger share of the funding each year. One requirement
would be for the grantee to identify local funding sources
early in the developmental process.

Project planning. --Most projects were well conceived
and well planned through the end of the developmental stage.
However, there was a noticeable gap in planning for the
transition from developmental to operational status. In addition to the question of funding, which has already been discussed, formal plans dealing with a way in which an innovative project may be merged with regular operations rarely
existed. For example, reference staff were not prepared
to work with a computer information system, even though a
library's administration might intend for reference librarians
to assume this responsibility. Although staff educational
programs had occasionally been conceptualized, rarely were
formal programs of instruction visible.

Introducing a new activity within a library's existing
organization structure also creates problems. Some projects
were administered outside the regular library chain of command. This approach seemed to succeed so long as the
project did not require the services of other library units.
Unfortunately, most projects cannot long exist in isolation.

Library planning was somewhat hampered whenever a
project was administered by a person not associated directly
with the library. A few projects were directed by researchers attached to units other than the library, e. g. , the
computer center, an information science department, or
another academic teaching department. All too often the director failed to involve the campus library sufficiently in
project planning, even though it was understood that the library would assume responsibility for the system once it
became operational. Under such circumstances, a library
was not always provided with sufficient lead time to plan for
an orderly transfer of activity. These non-library project
directors were committing the same error as had their librarian counterparts from other projects. The reassess-
ments necessitated by programs such as the ARL Management Review and Analysis Program may ameliorate some
planning problems generated by today's innovative projects.

Creating a More Receptive Environment
for Library Innovation

        There are several ways a library administrator can
stimulate a more receptive environment for innovation. Several guidelines emerged from the data collected during this
study:

        1.   Library administrators must be committed to the
innovative undertaking. A commitment from the chief administrator is essential, if stable funding is to be expected, and
if the organizational transition from experimental to operational status is to be successfully weathered. Furthermore,
the parent institution itself must be committed to the funding
of the innovation. This is particularly important when existing funding patterns within the institution will be affected by
the project.

        2.   A library's staff should be encouraged to partici-
pate in the project as early as possible. They must understand how the project might affect existing library services
and procedures. It must be remembered that the staff may
not view a project employing the computer with the same
sanguinity as the system's developers. To them the project
may lead to their professional obsolescence. If a project is
likely to affect existing procedures, the administrators should
be prepared to take steps to ensure that dislocation of staff
members is minimized. The potential adverse staff reaction
to some new systems underscores the critical need for
thorough preparatory planning.

        3.   The information needs of users should be given
careful consideration. A concerted effort to involve users
in the development of local information processing systems
should be made. Users should be invited to outline their information requirements. Efforts should be made to generate
interest and secure commitments long before the system becomes operational.

        4.   The library should be prepared to train users to
use the new service. One cannot assume that faculty and researchers are familiar with existing library services.[25,26]
Moreover, the information needs of users do not remain
static. A service which provides additional access points to
information will produce new and different user aspirations.[27]
This phenomenon was also observed in a study of attitudes
toward document delivery services. The typical faculty

member tended to evaluate document delivery as a frill, too
costly for the library to maintain. But after using the service one or more times, his attitude became much more positive because the service assumed a greater relevance to his
work. [28]

    5. New services should be marketed by the library.
Some do not approve of marketing programs because they
feel such activities are contradictory to the tone of academe.
Nevertheless, a library which wishes to sell a new program
must first acquaint potential users with the benefits of the
new service if it is to gain general campus acceptance.

    6. Administrators should develop a formal plan which
outlines the way in which a new service will be made operational. Experience derived from many current projects reveals that considerable time will be required before stable
funding is insured. Therefore, a plan should be prepared as
early as possible.

Concluding Observations

    Although the investigation was not designed to survey
all types of library innovations, a variety of projects were
visited. Based upon data collected, several general observations seem appropriate.

    1. There is now greater effort to focus library ser-
vices on the needs of individual researchers, e.g., individual
SDI profiles as opposed to the traditional services geared to
the needs of large groups of undifferentiated users, such as
interlibrary loan and general reference services.

    2. Computerized information services are designed
primarily to serve faculty and researchers. The value of
these specialized systems to undergraduate and graduate students has not yet been fully recognized.

    3. Librarians do not agree on how to use data in
machine-readable form to produce bibliographical finding
lists. Bibliographical tools currently proposed by some researchers could produce profound changes in library service
and library use patterns.

    4. The variety of formats in machine-readable rec-
ords currently used by libraries could retard the development

of regional and national networks.   Records in machine-readable form are still largely unique to local environments.
They are not easily transported to other machine environments, and there is still little evidence that data in machine formats are exchanged extensively on a regular basis among groups of institutions.

5.   Discipline-oriented information systems have proliferated on campuses during the past ten years.   Librarians usually are not directly involved in the development of these systems, but they could serve an important function as "information processing consultants or brokers" to researchers who must store, process and retrieve data.

6.   As accessibility to bibliographic data improves, greater emphasis will have to be placed on improving the physical accessibility of documents.   Data without documents will only further exacerbate current dissatisfactions of library users.

7.   One benefit to today's innovative systems may not be the systems' immediate impact, but rather the long-range changes they render on the current library environment. Today's innovations may create library environments which are more hospitable to further innovative undertakings.   In economic terms, a multiplier effect may be generated.

8.   Librarians need to become more sensitive to the importance of marketing.   Also, instructional programs are necessary to acquaint and educate users to the potential value of new systems.

9.   Librarians are beginning to reassess traditional organizational objectives and current program priorities in order to measure the importance of new programs in relation to traditional activities.   Objective setting is particularly critical during the current period of stable budgets.   Most new services can be introduced only at the expense of some existing program.

10.   It is often stated that librarians are generally reluctant to adopt new solutions to problems.   However, at no time during the project did the surveyor sense any unwillingness to adopt new techniques.   What may have been lacking among those interviewed was the experience to achieve objectives at minimum cost.   Most administrators would benefit from greater exposure to other on-going

library projects. Designers should be provided more opportunities to share their experiences with others contemplating
similar undertakings. Librarians would be more willing to
adopt new ideas if they understood fully the potential value
of the innovation to their library.

Notes

1. Arthur M. McAnally and Robert B. Downs. "The
   Changing Role of Directors of University Libraries,"
   College and Research Libraries 34:123-5, 1973.

2. Duane F. Webster. "The Management Review and
   Analysis Program: An Assisted Self-Study to Secure Constructive Change in the Management of
   Research Libraries," College and Research Libraries 35:114-25, 1974.

3. California, Program Review Branch, Audits Division,
   Department of Finance, Library Cooperation: A
   Systems Approach to Interinstitutional Resource
   Utilization, Report and Recommendations. Sacra-
   mento, June 1973. Report No. PR-70. 75p. (The
   sweeping indictments expressed in the report embody
   many misstatements, over-simplifications and biases,
   but the report does reflect the kind of dissatisfactions toward library management which are too commonly voiced by governmental officials.)

4. Everett M. Rogers. Diffusion of Innovations. New
   York, The Free Press of Glencoe, 1962, p. 13.
   (Rogers had defined innovation as "... an idea perceived as new by the individual. It really matters
   little, as far as human behavior is concerned,
   whether or not the idea is objectively new as measured [by the] amount of time elapsed since its first
   use or discovery. It is the newness of the idea to
   the individual that determines his reaction.")

5. An institution was selected for a visit when it became
   known that the library was engaged in an innovative
   project. The list of libraries visited is appended.
   The persons interviewed were usually directly involved with the specific project. Whenever possible,
   the director of the library was interviewed. Although
   some directors were intimately involved, other

directors confined their participation to general
managerial concerns ranging from funding to future
staffing ramifications. Interviews were generally
open-ended in format in order to encourage the inter-
viewees to express their own perceptions of the project. However, each interview session included several standard topics: 1) objectives of the project,
2) targeted user populations, 3) sources of funding,
4) evaluative techniques, 5) special features of the
system, and 6) advice which the project director
might offer to others undertaking similar projects.

6. Although many projects were observed, only the ones
   considered most significant as related to this survey
   are cited in this paper.

7. Donald J. Hillman and Andrew J. Kasarda. "The
   LEADER Retrieval System," [Proceedings of the]
   Spring Joint Computer Conference, 1969, p. 447-55.

8. James L. Carmon. "A Campus-Based Information
   Center," Special Libraries 64:65-9, 1973.

9. Peter G. Watson and R. Bruce Briggs. "Computerized
   Information Services for the University Community,"
   Information Storage and Retrieval 8:21-33, 1972.

10. The systems observed at the University of Pittsburgh
    and Ohio State University were similar to the ones
    cited, but they were not as fully developed at the
    time of visit in 1971.

11. Peter H. Rohn. "The United Nations Treaty Series
    Project," International Studies Quarterly 12:174-95,
    1968 (June).

12. Patricia Paylore. Arid Lands Research at the Univer-
    sity of Arizona. Tucson, University of Arizona,
    1974.

13. A. Callaghan and others. Students' Chemical Informa-
    tion Project, Oct. 1967-Sept. 1968, Final Report.
    (Copies available from the Office of Scientific and
    Technical Information, Department of Education and
    Science, Elizabeth House, York Road, London S. F. 1.)

14. Bath University of Technology, University Library.

Experimental Information Officer in the Social
Sciences, Report on work carried out in 1969.
1970, 50p.

15. Jack B. King. The Hamline Project, an educational
     information system for the small college campus.
     St. Paul, Minnesota, 1974. 17p.; and Implementing
     an Undergraduate Information System Based on the
     Hamline Model. St. Paul, Minnesota, 1974. 15p.
     Final report and Supplement to the ... National
     Science Foundation. (GN-873.1)

16. Irene B. Hoadley and A. Robert Thorson, eds. An
     Automated On-Line Circulation System: Evaluation,
     Development, Use; Proceedings and Papers of an
     Institute Held at the Ohio State University, Septem-
     ber 13-4, 1971. Columbus, The Library, 1973.
     85p.

17. Robin W. MacDonald and J. McRee Elrod. "An Ap-
     proach to Developing Computer Catalogs," College
     and Research Libraries 34:202-8, 1973.

18. Richard M. Dougherty. "The Evaluation of a Campus
     Library Document Delivery Service," College and
     Research Libraries 34:29-39, 1973.

19. Callaghan and others, op. cit.

20. Jack B. King, op. cit.

21. Richard M. Dougherty and Laura Blomquist. Improving
     Access to Library Resources: The Influence of Or-
     ganization of Library Collections, and of User Atti-
     tudes Toward Innovative Services. Metuchen, New
     Jersey, Scarecrow Press, 1974.

22. Derrick John de Solla Price. Little Science, Big
     Science. New York, Columbia University Press,
     1963.

23. Rogers, op. cit., p. 15-18.

24. H. William Axford. "Performance Measurement Re-
     visited," College and Research Libraries 34:249-57,
     1973.

25. Jerold Nelson. "Faculty Awareness and Attitudes
    Toward Academic Library Reference Services: A
    Measure of Communication," College and Research
    Libraries 34:268-75, 1973.

26. Lawrence E. Leonard and others. Centralized Book
    Processing: A Feasibility Study Based on Colorado
    Academic Libraries. Metuchen, N.J., Scarecrow
    Press, 1969, p. 211-43.

27. Edwin Parker. "Behavioral Research in the Develop-
    ment of a Computer-based Information System," in
    C. Nelson and D. Pollock, eds. Communication
    Among Scientists and Engineers. Lexington, Mass.,
    Heath Lexington Books, 1970, p. 281-93.

28. Dougherty and Blomquist, op. cit.

INSTITUTIONS VISITED

University of Nice. Science Library	October 21, 1970
Deutsche Forschungsgemeinschaft,	October 23, 1970
Bad Godesberg, Germany	
Bibliotheck Technische Hogeschool,	October 24, 1970
Delft, The Netherlands	
British National Bibliography	October 28, 1970
Bath Institute of Technology. Library	October 30, 1970
Bodleian Library. Oxford University	October 31, 1970
University of Birmingham, Library	November 2, 1970
National Lending Library, Boston	November 4, 1970
Spa, Great Britain	
University of Newcastle. Library	November 5, 1970
University of Dublin. Trinity	November 9, 1970
College Library	
Lehigh University. Library and	Jan. 7-8, 1971
Institute of Information Science	
University of Georgia. Library and	Jan. 25-26, 1971
Computer Center	
Georgia Tech University. Library	January 27, 1971
School of Information Science	
University of Pittsburgh. Library	February 9, 1971
Ohio State University. Library and	Feb. 22-23, 1971
School of Computer and Information	
Science	
University of Colorado. Library	Feb. 24, 1971
Hamline University, St. Paul,	March 1-2, 1971
Minn. Library	

University of Toronto. Library	March 3, 1971
Oklahoma State Library	March 14-15, 1971
University of Arizona. Library, Arid	March 16-17, 1971
Lands Information Center, and Tree Ring Research Project	
Arizona State University. Library	March 18, 1971
University of California, Berkeley. Library	March 21-22, 1971
Stanford University. Communication School and the Library	March 22-23, 1971
University of Washington. Library, Library School and United Nations Treaty Service	March 24, 1971
University of British Columbia. Library and the Poison Control Center	March 25-26, 1971
University of California, Los Angeles. Library, Institute of Library Research, and the Campus Computing Network	June 3-4, 1971
University of California, Riverside. Library	June 4, 1971

SCHOLARS IN RESIDENCE

Ira W. Harris

One of Ralph Shaw's favorite schemes was the notion
of bringing teachers and students together in the library, in
an informal joint quest for knowledge and ideas. When he
left Rutgers to return to library administration in 1965, he
created the opportunity to experiment with this scheme. The
following account is a record of that experiment. It is also
testimony to Shaw's originality and resourcefulness and to
the range of his interests; the record implies a humanistic
concern not always obvious in some of his other pursuits.

Shaw left Rutgers to become Dean of Library Activities at the University of Hawaii in 1965. Under this title
he took on simultaneously the tasks of founding a library
school and developing a university library system. Within
a span of about three years, he had accomplished substantially all of both endeavors. The school was accredited and
its graduates were occupying professional positions in Hawaii,
on the mainland and in Asia; the library's collections were
reclassified from Dewey to LC, its professional personnel
were moved from civil service to faculty status, a new graduate research library was completed and staffed on the subject divisional plan, and a separate undergraduate library
had been created by renovation of the former campus main
library.

Sinclair Undergraduate Library opened with a new
65,000-volume collection, selected with special attention to
the needs of undergraduates, and with a dial-access listening
and viewing center for the use of nonprint media under con-
struction. It was not, however, the physical resources of
the new undergraduate library that marked its emergence as
a going concern, but rather a strong service philosophy and
program. Shaw's own convictions contributed much to this

44

orientation, just as any institution becomes an extension of
its leader's image. The foundations of the service program
were developed under a pilot project conceived by Shaw and
funded by the Carnegie Corporation.

The Carnegie grant underwrote an experimental approach to library services for undergraduates, envisioned as
a means of encouraging self-generating, lifelong learning.
Its primary target was the average student--not the marginal
pupil nor the brilliant one--who does well enough to get by,
but is substantially ignored because he neither does so badly
as to need extra attention nor so well as to attract it.   In
this regard, the project was a kind of grand extension of
Shaw's personal interaction with his own students. He had
a way of getting more out of them than they thought they
were able to give. Similarly, his concern in the project was
to help students realize their full potential, or at least come
closer to it. It would be silly to contend that many students
were so specifically affected by the library's services. Yet
Shaw's visionary approach gave impetus and tone to the project, and fostered a climate for innovation and change.   The
scholar-in-residence program was one of several experiments
in library service that were initiated by Shaw and supported
by the Carnegie grant.

The concept was simple. A professor or scholar
would be available in the library to converse informally with
students, to talk about ideas and the resources that contained
them. It was not a new concept; advocates of the library-
college would have been quite at home with it, and in fact
they have traced the origins of something of the sort back
through the centuries.[1] The notion of professors serving in
the library as benign bibliographic guides was implemented
in the 1920's in some American colleges.[2,3] Except for
special programs, however, such as poetry readings or similar structured presentations, no variation of the practice
has become widespread. The Hawaii experiment remains
relatively unusual as a contemporary example of this idea.

The Scholar-in-Residence Program was essentially an
experiment in encouraging students to read and think for
themselves, through informal discussion of books and ideas
with scholars in various fields. Intellectual stimulation is
presumed to be a normal feature of the college environment,
but the classroom experience does not necessarily guarantee
it for all, and many average students miss the encourage-
ment of self-directed inquiry that a busy faculty may give

outside the class to a few of the most promising. The program sought, therefore, to assure the free access of all students to challenging individual encounters with active minds, on topics of the student's own choice. The library had special qualifications as a setting: it was intimately related to the learning enterprise but essentially independent of curricular structure; it was the obvious and inexhaustible source for independent acquisition of new knowledge; it was neutral ground, freely accessible to all categories and kinds of students, yet lacking the formality of the faculty office.

Three scholars participated in the program, the first for three months of the Spring 1966 semester, the other two for six weeks each during the Fall of 1966. Publicity was necessary to inform students what the program was all about, yet the project staff wanted to find out whether the students would use such a service if it was simply available, as distinguished from a service that was intensively sold to them. Publicity therefore was intentionally limited. Each person was the subject of at least three local newspaper stories and of a display in the library. Each achieved outside exposure as well, appearing before student and other community groups, and participating in radio or television programs in which the Scholar-in-Residence Program at the University Library was referred to. All three had books of their own in print and on hand at the time of the experiment.

Dr. Houston Peterson, a retired philosophy professor from Rutgers University, former director of the Cooper Union Forum, author, anthologist, and sometime radio and television personality, was available to students every afternoon at a table in the corner of the library lobby. The location was deliberately public, yet offered at the same time a kind of privacy in its crowded, busy surroundings. Dr. Peterson's talent for what he called the Art of Conversation and his passion for books were his special qualifications. Indeed, he seemed made for the bibliographic part of the job; "Peterson doesn't just read a book," a colleague once said of him, "He possesses it. He scribbles in the margins, underlines, writes himself notes. He loves words, he bathes daily in them and scrubs his teeth with them.... He's always buying books, haunting second-hand bookstores in New York, lugging a briefcase full of books around campus and giving books away to favorite people."[4]

Conversations with students, usually one at a time, could be seen taking place whenever Dr. Peterson was on

duty, and it was evident that he was meeting some degree of
acceptance.   To learn something about what was really hap-
pening in these interviews and about the kinds of students
reached, several techniques were used.   Whenever it seemed
possible to do so casually, Dr. Peterson wrote down students'
names and whatever he could inconspicuously set down or
later recall about the conversations.   The resultant sample
was made available for subsequent contact and background
investigation.   Additional insight into the nature of this first
attempt was sought through the use of a questionnaire mailed
to the recorded sample in the month following the conclusion
of Dr. Peterson's tour of duty.   The questionnaire had the
virtue of stimulating a good deal of free commentary.   Despite some negative reactions, the participants were unani-
mously in favor of continuing the Scholar-in-Residence program.   Seventy-five per cent stated that they were encouraged by the experience to do more reading.

        Faculty attitudes toward the program were favorable,
as evidenced by occasional commentary and a few commen-
datory letters.   The major indication of faculty and administration approval was the development of joint support for
the next scholar, whose appointment called for six weeks as
Library Scholar-in-Residence and the remainder of a semester as Visiting Lecturer in the Speech Department.

        Dr. Everett Lee Hunt, an authority on classical rhe-
toric and retired Dean of Students at Swarthmore College,
arrived the following semester.   His recent book, The Re-
volt of The College Intellectual, and his long career at
Swarthmore as Dean and mentor of students were considered
to be his special qualifications.

        Dean Hunt occupied the same location and employed
the same technique of occasionally transcribing the name of
the student and later the substance of the discussion.   Dean
Hunt's record of individual interviews was considerably more
detailed than Dr. Peterson's, and it was clear from his
records and from the steady response that the program was
functioning much as intended, even more so, perhaps, than
in the first instance.   It was concluded, therefore, that
while another questionnaire might bring further endorsement
of the program, it would not contribute much further understanding of the phenomenon itself.

        John S. Wilson, jazz music critic of the New York
Times, author of three definitive works on jazz, and an

occasional contributor on that subject to popular magazines,
was the third scholar.   He differed from the others in having
had very little previous formal contact with the academic
world.   The nature of his specialty and its obvious appeal to
the younger generation were considered his special qualifications for the job.

Mr. Wilson's sessions with students differed markedly
from those of his predecessors.   He was in a somewhat
more secluded location, in the fourth floor Honors Reading
Room.   He was equipped with a basic collection of jazz records and a phonograph, and he played selections whenever
he or the students felt like listening.   He was closely identified with a single, popular, non-academic interest, and his
sessions often consisted of listening to jazz and discussing
jazz with whole groups of students.   Personal or academic
problems or other interests received less attention, and
whereas the previous scholars infrequently met with more
than one person at a time, Wilson's sessions involved anywhere from one or two to 25 or 30 people.   He was also
able to record a sampling of student names.

The attendance record and the demand for Wilson that
quickly arose on campus from student organizations were in-
dicators of student acceptance and enthusiasm.   The demand
for the basic record list and the concern of students about
the future disposition of the record collection were additional
evidence of interest.

Project staff assembled background information[5] on
the partial list of students who participated in the Scholar-
in-Residence Program.   Many qualifications must accompany
the data assembled.   The gathering of student identities was
dependent on the scholars' assessments of how much it would
impinge on the atmosphere of the interview;   owing to internal problems in the University registration office, data was
unavailable for some names;   and information taken from
Bureau of Student Activities files was originally recorded by
the students themselves but unedited.   Of a total estimated
population for the whole program of about 600 participants,
only 239 were listed, and data were finally assembled on
only 166.   Thus the emergent picture of the kinds of students
who availed themselves of this unusual service is probably
inaccurate in some respects.

It can be said, however, that there was student representation from all major academic divisions or colleges,

from at least 30 different major subject disciplines, and from
all class levels, and that there were faculty and outside participants as well.   Less than a dozen students were identified
who talked with more than one scholar.   From available records, it would appear that undergraduates were in the majority, though graduate students were more heavily represented (over one-fourth) in proportion to their total in the
whole student body.   Mean and median grade point ratios for
listed students were within the middle range at 2.8.   It
would also appear that participants in the program differed
from the students at large in the following ways: they were
less apt to be living at home, more apt to have mainland
origins, more apt to have some sort of employment while
attending college, three times as likely to belong to one or
more student organizations of one kind or another.   Again,
the data on which these tentative conclusions rest are
sketchy, and the proportion of graduate students further
colors the results.   However, it seems obvious that the program was no general haven for the withdrawn malcontent,
nor the lonely genius;   there is at least some indication that
these students were a little above average in scholarship and
in participation in campus activities.

        True measures of the program's effectiveness elude
any statistical descriptions.   Whether the interviews met a
need, whether they did encourage students to read and think
for themselves, and to continue to use books and libraries
creatively--whether the students really understood these con-
cepts--can best be judged, perhaps, by the commentary of
those involved.   While there were many criticisms of procedure and some reservations about the personality of one
of the scholars, there was widespread endorsement of the
idea, and an apparent understanding of its basic purposes.
Students commented:

> This type of discussion is essentially good because
> it is not restricted by inhibitions which may arise
> out of a relation in a teacher-student talk.   Stu-
> dents at times feel inhibited in discussing intellec-
> tual matters with a teacher under whom a course
> is being taken at the moment.

> I think that there can be more honest expression
> of ideas on a wider range of topics than in a pro-
> fessor-student relationship.   The conversations I
> had were exhilarating.

I'd still rather have someone to talk to than merely
to read sentiments I agree with. If I may gener-
alize from my own experience, college students
are finding themselves, or at least the sensitive
ones are. They need desperately someone to try
out their new ideas on. They need a chance to
articulate what they feel, so that they can systema-
tize it ... they need someone to listen, and no one
has time to listen. And so they do not articulate,
and they do not find themselves, and they become
frustrated without knowing why.... What is needed
is a personal contact and a dedication to self ful-
fillment.

I don't think a student will do more reading unless
he feels that he'll get something from it. The
scholar ought to be so enthusiastic or present such
challenges, either by opening up new horizons or
making the student feel that there is a vast unex-
plored region, that he will use books to find out
about it.... I think it ought to be a person that
makes you think, myself.

Since the faculty as such are, or seem to be, too
busy to take on talking to the individuals who want
to, it seems to me imperative to provide someone
to do specifically that. One of the reasons students often show such lack of interest in their
studies is simply a reflection they get from their
teachers. One of the foremost ways of learning
is through interaction with those who know more
than you. The scholar has a kind of enthusiasm
about reading and learning (apart from a job to
make money or a course which must be conducted
and evaluated) which makes reading its own reward,
so to speak. 6

The scholars said:

And now, looking back on this 'pilot' experience
... when I talked informally with scores of undergraduates, graduates, non-students, etc. , I am
convinced that this kind of ambiguous position has
enormous possibilities in our expanding colleges
and universities....

Although it may not have been part of the original

intent in engaging the scholar that his horizons
would be broadened by the experience, this has
turned out to be the case. This has occurred not
only in putting the scholar in intimate touch with
the attitudes of the contemporary college generation
toward jazz. The most striking result has been
that the scholar has heard recordings that he is
familiar with with fresh ears--he has gained an appreciation of aspects of recordings that he never had
before because he was able to listen to them in
the company of this particular audience and to respond both as part of the group and to their responses.

As a means of focusing attention on library activities that are meaningful to the entire campus and
to the surrounding community, this type of scholar-
in-residence program could be repeated to advantage, using other aspects of the creative arts.

They seem to show a longing to talk and to be
heard, but a good deal of hesitancy about making
the approach.... A number mentioned that they
did not like to go to counselors and were not
pleased when they did, because the job seemed to
be somewhat professionalized and formalized, and
the interviews were quite short, with the counselor
taking the initiative. Talk about books seemed to
arise out of their own account on how they came to
hold certain views and attitudes. They appreciated
mention of books which developed subjects in which
they were already interested. Very few of the
number were interested in the choice of a career
from the point of view of getting the best paid job,
but seemed to be looking mostly for inner satisfaction. They seemed to be thoughtful and intelligent
people who did not need to have interest aroused
in books, they already had that, but seemed to ap-
preciate talking with someone who had experienced
similar problems and who had in one way or
another survived them. The whole experience was
interesting and rewarding for me.... [7]

Although a fourth scholar, John Jacob Niles, was
jointly sponsored by the Library and the Music Department
during the year following completion of the pilot project,
the library's program was eventually discontinued. It was

a casualty of rapidly escalating enrollment and the increasing
investment of administrative and staff time in orientation and
reference services. The pressures responsible for its dis-
appearance resurrect a dilemma long familiar to college librarians: when the preponderance of academic library use
is course-related, and when this use requires strong library
support with reference and other basic services, how can the
promotion of non-course reading--and thinking--be justified?
Yet the world has changed, and current views of what constitutes an authentic learning experience are perhaps more
enlightened. Higher education today offers more options to
students than were generally available seven years ago. Innovative techniques in the classroom as well as new learning
opportunities outside in the community provide a diversified
learning environment. Conceivably, scholars in library
residence are a viable addition to this environment. Once
again, Shaw may have been a little ahead of his time.

                              Notes

1. Robert T. Jordan. "The 'Library-College,' A Merging
    of Library and Classroom" in (Dan) Bergen, ed.
    Libraries and the College Climate of Learning.
    Syracuse, Syracuse University Press, 1966, pp. 52-3.

2. In 1924 the president of Rollins College "established the
    first Professorship of Books in America.... How
    many thousands of college students have longed for a
    sort of omniscient, sympathetic, and versatile li-
    brarian and teacher who would be able to direct not
    only classroom but recreational reading!" R. S.
    Clark. "Book Consciousness in a College," Library
    Journal 56:72-4, 1931.

3. "The plan was tried ... of having the professors come
    to the library and sit in the reference room to an-
    swer questions and offer necessary suggestions for
    effective work. A few tried it but do not like it.
    It is too hard work. The students profited but the
    instructors said it was wearing work and ceased to
    come." P. L. Windsor. "Report of the Illinois
    Library Association Meeting, College and Reference
    Section, October 27-29, 1927," Libraries 32:550-1,
    1927.

4. "Houston Peterson, A Great Teacher," Report From
    Rutgers 15:2, June 1963.

5. Data compiled from student files in Office of Admissions
    and Records. University of Hawaii; from card files
    in the Bureau of Student Activities Office, University
    of Hawaii; and from the Institutional Research Office
    publications, University of Hawaii Student Survey(s),
    Fall 1964 and Fall 1966.

6. Quotations are from anonymous returns of the Scholar-
    in-Residence Program Student Questionnaire, May,
    1966.

7. Quotations are from final reports submitted by the
    scholars to the project staff.

THE REAL WORLD OF CONTINUING EDUCATION FOR LIBRARY PERSONNEL

Peter Hiatt

It started in Wyoming in 1964, when Joseph Shubert, who had just moved to ALA Headquarters from his position as Nevada State Librarian, conducted a two-day "community study" workshop for public library personnel sponsored by the Wyoming State Library. Two out-of-staters attended. In 1965, then an Associate Professor at the Graduate Library School, Indiana University, and Public Library Consultant for the Indiana State Library, I ran a five-day credit workshop for the Wyoming State Library on "adult services" for public, school and community college library personnel. Four out-of-staters attended. In 1966, Mildred Young Johnson, on the faculty of the Graduate School of Library Service, Rutgers University, gave a "scientific management" seminar, and I did a one-day follow-up clinic on my previous year's Wyoming Adult Services Institute. More out-of-staters attended each of these. It became apparent to all that the quality of the sessions was enhanced by the mix of in- and out-of-state personnel, and that the Wyoming State Library was putting together continuing education programs of value to neighboring states. It was also becoming apparent to Andy Fisher, then Wyoming State Librarian, that the material, personnel, and fiscal resources of a single state were being stretched to the utmost. If the Wyoming pattern of continuing education programs was to continue and to be of increasing benefit, several states would have to be involved in the planning and support.

A meeting was called early in 1967, and I was asked to give a brief presentation on continuing education needs. By the end of that full-day meeting in Cheyenne, several states had agreed that they should form a consortium to conduct continuing education programs designed to meet the

special needs of sparsely settled states. The group then
turned to the Western Interstate Commission for Higher Education (WICHE) for help.

WICHE is a nonprofit agency created by the thirteen
western states in 1951. The commission operates under the
Western Regional Education Compact, which is an agreement
among the states to work cooperatively to improve educational programs and facilities. Program activity began in
1953, and WICHE currently administers more than fifty programs to improve higher education in the West. Among
these are: the Mountain States Regional Medical Programs,
Continuing Psychiatric Education for Physicians, Continuing
Education Programs for Nurses, Improvement of Nursing
Curricula, Planning Resources in Minority Education, the
Student Exchange Programs, the National Center for Higher
Education Management Systems at WICHE, the Western Con-
ference on the Uses of Mental Health Data, Resources De-
velopment Internship Programs, Mountain States Community
College Consortium, and the Corrections Program.

WICHE agreed to coordinate a study to identify the
continuing education needs of librarians in all types of libraries in the West, to identify educational resources, and
to develop a plan to implement a continuing education program to meet the identified educational needs. The state
library agencies of Alaska, Arizona, Colorado, Idaho,
Nevada, New Mexico, Washington and Wyoming funded the
study. In the summer of 1968, WICHE set up an office
under the leadership of Barbara Conroy and hired a three-
person team to conduct the survey: Dr. Lawrence A. Allen,
Dean, School of Library Science, University of Kentucky;
Dr. Robert E. Lee, then Chairman, Department of Librarianship, Kansas State Teachers College; and myself at that
time Associate Professor, Graduate Library School, Indiana
University, and Library Consultant, Indiana State Library.

The team surveyed the needs for continuing education
of all levels of library personnel and interested laymen and
conducted extensive interviews and group sessions with
leaders from all types of libraries and information centers
in each of the thirteen states served by WICHE. The report, A Plan for Developing a Program of Continuing Education for Library Personnel (1969), lists the major continuing
education needs found, notes significant similarities among
the Western states, and recommends a structure for meeting
those needs. Specifically, the authors found that methodology

of presentation and experimentation with a variety of workshop formats need a good deal of emphasis. Training the
trainers was seen as the key to an eventual breakthrough in
this multistate effort. WICHE was seen as the most suitable
agency to coordinate the program, with state library agencies
as the most appropriate location for statewide responsibility
and multistate cooperation.

In the fall of 1970, I was employed by the Western
Interstate Commission for Higher Education as Director of
the new program and charged with the responsibility to seek
funds to support a multistate continuing education program
for library personnel in the West.

At the first meeting of the program's National Advisory Committee in January 1971,[1] as Director I was advised to devote all of my efforts to securing outside funds
for the program. That proved to be an error, as it grad-
ually became clear that outside funding was not easily obtainable for many reasons. At the same time, programming
efforts suffered. When it became necessary to turn back
for funding to the state library agencies themselves, there
was no concrete way to answer the questions of a few who
felt they could not fund a program which had not actually
demonstrated its value. Two state agencies withdrew their
commitment to the program. But six (Alaska, Arizona,
Colorado, Montana, Nevada and Washington) continued their
support.

The eighteen months of fund-seeking had included
many interviews and letters of intent or proposals submitted
to the Kellogg Foundation, Council on Library Resources,
National Endowment for the Arts and Humanities, Xerox
Fund, several local and Western foundations, and the Bureau
of Libraries and Educational Technology. With the exception
of the Xerox Fund, none was able to fund any aspect of the
program.[2] Xerox contributed $12,000 to support training.

In December 1972, the Western Council on Continuing
Education for Library Personnel was created. Its charter
was approved by the Commissioners of the Western Interstate Commission for Higher Education (WICHE). The responsibilities assigned to the Director by the Western Council were:

    1. To identify the continuing education needs of li-
        brary personnel in the participating states;

2. To create or adapt continuing education programs
    and packages which can meet those needs;
3. To mount or deliver and evaluate these programs
    and packages;
4. To seek outside funding to build on core funding
    from the participating states.

The charter members were the state library agencies
of Alaska, Arizona, Montana, Nevada, and Washington.
Mrs. Ruth Hamilton, Consultant in Continuing Education,
Washington State Library, was elected chairman of the Council, and Mrs. Marguerite Cooley, Director, Arizona State
Department of Library and Archives, was elected vice-chairman. Using a formula combining a basic fee of $5,200 with
a per capita fee of $0.005, income from the states for the
first year was $60,000.[3] In January 1973, the Xerox Fund
contributed $12,000 for the "retraining of library personnel,"
bringing the year's budget to $72,000. In February 1974,
the Council voted that a maximum fee of $15,000 per year
be levied for all new states joining the Program, and that
fees for charter members whose formula contribution was
above $15,000 be reduced to this level as soon as practi-
cable.

Benefits

The benefits of having a group of states working together, sharing resources and know-how, are apparent. The
WICHE Western Council on Continuing Education for Library
Personnel is a unique multistate effort in library continuing
education. A multistate consortium means greater and more
diverse human and institutional resources. WICHE adds experience, know-how, and contacts from more than twenty
years of work with educational agencies in the thirteen
Western states. WICHE offers strong supporting services,
including computerized budgeting and accounting, complete
printing and duplicating services, and a fiscal staff with long
experience in managing federal and foundation funds. WICHE
also has excellent physical facilities, including office space
and complete conference facilities. Many of WICHE's programs are parallel to or relate directly to library needs
and interests.

Multistate continuing education events bring participants the additional benefits of sharing and testing ideas,
experiences, problems, and solutions with other library

EDUCATIONAL MATRIX
(Continuing Education Building Blocks)

The Western Council on Continuing Education for Library Personnel
WESTERN INTERSTATE COMMISSION FOR HIGHER EDUCATION

MANAGERS AND MIDDLE MANAGERS All Types of Libraries	REFERENCE SERVICES All Types of Libraries	ADULT SERVICES All Types of Libraries	LIBRARY MATERIALS	TRUSTEES
Staff Development Consultation		Public Relations for Library and Lay Leaders	A Community Librarian's Training Program	LEADS
Utilization of Library Manpower	Government Documents Workshop Kit	Public Relations for Staff	Non-Print Materials Seminar	How to Hire A Librarian
Dynamic Library Management (MBO)	Reference: The User, Interview, The Tools	College Level Examination Program	A-V Services	Library Trusteeship: An Introduction
Problem Solving Workshop	Interlibrary Loan Workshop	Hispano Library Services		

Level of Staff Development Areas

Program Area for Each Program Area

Basic Foundation

FOUNDATION AND SUPPORTIVE EDUCATIONAL DEVELOPMENT PROGRAMS FOR ALL LEVELS AND ALL TYPES OF LIBRARIES:

☐ Staff Development and Continuing Education Programs for Library Personnel: Guidelines
☐ Interpersonal Communications Workshops
☐ Regional Personnel Educational Resources Development of Training Leadership and
☐ Student Exchange Program in Graduate Library Studies

NOTES: For a full presentation of regional library education needs, the program philosophy, activities and structure, see Lee, Allen, and Hiatt. A Plan for Developing a Regional Program of Continuing Education for Library Personnel. Boulder, Colorado, WICHE, 1969. Several of the above learning packages can fit into several categories.

environments.   State-level programs benefit not only from
being able to tap multistate resources, but also from activities pretested in other states.   Program developmental costs
are shared with other states.   The roadshow approach brings
both reduced development costs and lower costs per event.
Most importantly the Council members have been able to influence the development of library services in the West by
focusing on common needs.   One of the most useful products
of their work together in 1973 is the Educational Matrix
which guides the development of new educational packages so
that a logical building and continuity of programs is available
to both individuals and institutions.

        The matrix illustrates many of the concrete produc-
tions of the program to date.   These include the packages
Dynamic Library Management and Interpersonal Communications seminars, the slide-cassette kit titled Library Trusteeship, a large number of reference workshops, and special
publications of all kinds.   All of the WICHE-developed packages are delivered free to member states, and the cost of
the materials themselves is considerably reduced for members of the Council.   The publications developed include:

> Conroy, Barbara.   Staff Development and Continuing
> Education Programs for Library Personnel.
> Boulder, Colorado, Western Interstate Commis-
> sion for Higher Education, 1974.

> The Denver on Your Own Program.   Denver Public
> Library, Denver, Colorado.

> Hiatt, Peter and Noda, Octavio.   How to Hire a
> Librarian.   Boulder, Colorado, Western Inter-
> state Commission for Higher Education, 1974
> (slide/cassette).

> Hiatt, Peter and Noda, Octavio.   Library Trustee-
> ship: An Introduction.   Boulder, Colorado,
> Western Interstate Commission for Higher Edu-
> cation, 1972 (alide/cassette).

> LEADS: A Monthly Continuing Education Newsletter
> for Public Library Trustees (edited by Octavio
> Noda and Peter Hiatt).   Loveland, Colorado,
> Donars Publications.

> Shubert, Joseph F.   A Community Librarian's

Training Program. Boulder, Colorado, Western
Interstate Commission for Higher Education, 1973.

Vadala, Julia (Editor). Hispano Library Services for
Arizona, Colorado, and New Mexico (A Workshop
Held in Sante Fe, New Mexico, April 30, May 1-
2, 1970). Boulder, Colorado, Western Interstate
Commission for Higher Education, August 1970.

Quite a few continuing education packages were made
available to the member states. As they are field-tested,
refined, and used, an increasing number of them will be
made available to nonmember states in the West and elsewhere.

DYNAMIC LIBRARY MANAGEMENT: Management by
Objectives for Library Leaders

    2-1/2 Day Seminar, 3-5 Month At-Home Application,
      2-Day Follow-Up Clinic
    Leaders: Dr. Wes Handy, Management Consultant
                    Director, WICHE Continuing Education
                    Program for Library Personnel
    Participants: Managers and Middle Managers, All
                    Types of Libraries.

INTERPERSONAL COMMUNICATIONS WORKSHOP

    2-1/2 Day Workshop to Improve Written and Verbal
      Communications
    Leaders: Charles Hosford, National Training
                    Laboratories Consultant
                    Sue Buel, National Training Laboratories
                    Consultant
    Participants: All Levels of Personnel and Interested
                    Lay Leaders.

REFERENCE: The User, The Interview, The Tools

    2-1/2 Day, or Two One-Day Sequential Workshops
      Introducing Basic Reference Tools and Skills
    Leader: Mrs. Anne Mathews, kit developer,
                    will train area librarians in use of
                    the self-contained teaching kit as a
                    part of her commitment to offer the
                    workshop in each member state.
    Participants: Public and Reference Service Personnel

in All Types of Libraries. This is
an introductory course which can
also serve as a refresher.

UTILIZATION OF LIBRARY MANPOWER

2-Day Videotaped Seminar on Library Management
Leader: John Eastlick, Former Director, Den-
                ver Public Library and Professor,
                School of Librarianship, University
                of Denver
Participants: Managers and Middle Managers, All
                Types of Libraries.

IF WE DON'T HAVE IT, WE CAN GET IT FOR YOU

A Complete Kit for Presenting a One-Day Interlibrary
     Loan Workshop
Leaders: Trained or Approved by WICHE or
                State Library Agency Involved
Participants: All Personnel Dealing with the Public,
                All Types and Sizes of Libraries.

GOVERNMENT DOCUMENTS FOR THE USER

A Kit for Conducting a One-Day Workshop
Leader: To Be Trained or Approved by WICHE
                or the State Library Agency Involved
Participants: Public Service Personnel and Acquisi-
                tion Librarians, All Types of Li-
                braries--Introductory.

LIBRARY TRUSTEESHIP: AN INTRODUCTION

A Self-Contained 15-Minute Slide/Cassette Presentation
     for Trustees.

HOW TO HIRE A LIBRARIAN

A Self-Contained 15-minute Slide/Cassette Presenta-
     tion for Trustees.

Several Single Topic Seminars Designed
for Small Public Libraries

PUBLIC RELATIONS - A half-day seminar for public
     library professionals and trustees

PUBLIC RELATIONS - A half-day seminar for public
library staffs
NONPRINT MATERIALS SEMINAR - A 1-1/2 day
seminar to acquaint public library staff and
trustees with the practical aspects of nonprint
materials and services.
A-V SERVICES FOR THE PUBLIC LIBRARY - A half-
day presentation on workable ways of starting or
expanding a library AV program.

As the 1969 report noted, each of the thirteen Western
states shares the most significant continuing education needs.
These are needs for new knowledge and skills in the areas
of administrative abilities and managerial skills. These are
also needs to respond to the changing role of libraries and
changing patterns of library services. It was felt that such
important areas as basic library skills could be improved by
packaged programs developed centrally and administered locally. The key recommendation was for training the trainers
so that programs would have a built-in multiplier effect and
could be replicated with high quality at reduced costs. The
need to experiment with a variety of educational methods
(especially from the field of adult education) and media was
given high priority.

In July 1973, the Western Council approved budget for
FY 1974, putting WICHE's Continuing Education Program for
Library Personnel on a solid, financial base. The strength
and initial success of the program was reported by Mrs.
Ruth Hamilton, Chairman of the Western Council on Continuing Education for Library Personnel, in a session on the
program's progress at the annual meeting of the WICHE Commissioners in August 1973.

Purpose and Objectives

From the outset of the purpose of WICHE's multistate
Continuing Education Program for Library Personnel has been
to bring improvement in the delivery of library services in
the West through the vehicle of continuing education of all
levels of library personnel (and involved lay leaders) in all
types of libraries. The program has had the additional goals
of mounting and testing a variety of educational programs
using the most effective adult education methods and formats.

The program's components are: continuing education

events (management institutes, censorship workshops, communication seminars, information speeches); continuing education publications (such as the continuing education news-
letter for public library trustees, LEADS, and the recently
published Staff Development and Continuing Education Programs for Library Personnel aimed at all sizes and types of
library operations); and consultation related to the continuing
education of library and library related personnel (such as
advising in the design and evaluation of the 1972 Pacific
Northwest Library Association Conference, and the Mountain
Plains Library Association 1973 invitational self-evaluation
conference, and the staff development program at the University of Washington Libraries).

At its February 1974 meeting the Western Council on
Continuing Education for Library Personnel of WICHE, which
guides and funds the program, adopted a revised statement
of purpose:

> The Western Council on Continuing Education for
> Library Personnel shall deliver currently available
> continuing education programs for library-related
> personnel, identify new continuing education needs,
> and develop new resources to meet those needs.

> The Council seeks to strengthen cooperation among
> the Western states and between them and other re-
> gions to share library information resources, and
> hence to improve library services to all people
> through the West.

Impact of the Program

If one were to judge from the national interest and
attention given this regional program, the WICHE Continuing
Education Program for Library Personnel has made a successful start on its goal of serving as a model for similar
ventures in other regions.

What has been accomplished in the four years since
WICHE's Continuing Education Program for Library Personnel
was inaugurated?

First, and most importantly, a multistate program
has been established on a solid financial and professional
basis which allows for strong future development to meet
library change needs.

Second, the Western Council on Continuing Education
for Library Personnel has been formed as the basis for
guiding the program. Its charter has been accepted and supported by the WICHE Commissioners. Five dedicated states
have proved that a group of state library agencies can work
together effectively to improve library services not only in
their own states but also in the region.

Third, the program has tested methods and programs
designed to meet the immediate problems facing library development in the West. The program's activities have demonstrated that many library workers and leaders in all types
of libraries and at all levels of responsibility have an intense
desire to bring their public the best in library services and
materials, and they need only to recognize and sharpen their
own innate resources and abilities, which they have often
underestimated. With the simple incentive of "improvement
of the delivery of library services back home," a remarkable
number of librarians, library staffers, trustees, and lay
leaders have participated in a range of WICHE-generated continuing education programs.

The impact of this regional effort is best illustrated
by typical examples of library change which resulted from
the program's continuing education events, publications, and
consultation.

The first cooperative effort in one state to share collections among community college, county, and university libraries was the result of a specific project developed as an
assignment in the Dynamic Library Management Seminar
series.

A heavy increase in interlibrary loan activities and a
regional bibliographic center were the result of a series of
six, one-day workshops.

Mounting of a staff-run staff development program and
an immediate increase in participative management in two
university libraries was a result of WICHE-based consultation.

A measured increase in quantity and a subjectively
measured increase in quality in public library services to
Chicanos was a result of a workshop and subsequent publication, Hispano Library Services.

Elimination of outdated services and addition of

community-focused services by several public libraries was
a result of stimulation and ideas in <u>LEADS</u>.

A group of certified library aides have been able to
support statewide library development as a result of a cor-
respondence-discussion course designed and evaluated by
WICHE.

One state revised its five-year library plan as a by-
product of a one-day "Problem Solving Workshop. "

Realistic, on-going programs of shared collections
and community services between school and public libraries
were a result of a three-day "Interpersonal Communications
Workshop. "

The increase of accessibility to graduate library education for students in states without accredited library
schools, through WICHE's Student Exchange Program, is
another library program impact.

A revision of library management and administrative
methods in a large public library was a result of a "Management by Objectives Clinic. "

The funding of several new programs in public, special, community college, university, college, and school libraries was a result of WICHE continuing education efforts.

These examples are illustrative of the range and
variety of program impact, even though the program is relatively new.   The Council has asked that a means of quantitative measurement of program impact be developed.   Mean-
while, both the program director and the individual Council
members report regularly on changes in libraries resulting
from continuing education sponsored by WICHE.

Regionally the program has had an important role in
encouraging responsibility for quality, need-focused continuing
education for the Pacific Northwest Library Association, the
Mountain Plains Library Association, and all of the state library associations in the Council.   The evaluation of PNLA's
unique four-year focus on continuing education for its members was conducted by WICHE;   WICHE also participated in
the design of membership programs on the future of the
Mountain Plains Library Association.   Nationally, the program director was involved in many continuing education
activities.

The support of the Western Council on Continuing Education for Library Personnel has been predicated on a belief in experimentation with methodology and content, development and testing of continuing education packages, and the idea that states joining together can share resources to the benefit of themselves and the region. The program should be viewed by the profession as a prototype to be criticized and evaluated for possible adaptation to the needs of other regions.

Notes

1. The Members were: Mr. Richard B. Engen, Director, Division of State Libraries, Alaska State Library; Mrs. Marguerite B. Cooley, Director, Department of Library and Archives, State of Arizona; Mr. David Hoffman, then State Librarian, Montana State Library; Mr. Joseph J. Anderson, State Librarian, Nevada State Library; Mrs. Ruth Hamilton, Consultant in Continuing Education, Washington State Library; Dr. Lester Asheim, then Office for Library Education, American Library Association; Miss Mary V. Gaver, then Professor, Graduate School of Library Service, Rutgers University; Dean Margaret K. Goggin, Graduate School of Librarianship, University of Denver; Dr. Irving Lieberman, then Director, School of Librarianship, University of Washington.

2. Title IIB monies for institutes might have been available if the program had had the time and resources to work through a group of academic institutions to develop co-sponsored institute proposals. But the Advisory Committee felt that time spent seeking minigrants for specific institutes would leave little time for the multistate planning which would be the real strength of the program.

3. Using this formula ($5,200 + $0.005 per capita, 1970 census), the annual participation fees for the charter states were:

Alaska	$ 6,700
Arizona	14,055
Montana	8,672
Nevada	7,844
Washington	22,248

APPENDIX

Charter of the
Western Council on Continuing Education
for Library Personnel of the
Western Interstate Commission for Higher Education

The Western Interstate Commission for Higher Education
(hereinafter referred to as the Commission), recognizing the
need for regional development of continuing education for library personnel, has authorized the organization of a planning group to be known as the Western Council on Continuing
Education for Library Personnel (hereinafter referred to as
the Council).

I - FUNCTIONS

The functions of the Council shall be to:

Recommend to the Commission policies and priorities relating to continuing education for library personnel.

Provide a medium for exchange of ideas and sharing of
experiences by western state library agencies and institutions of higher education and other appropriate groups
which offer library education programs.

Identify needs with respect to continuing education in librarianship which need cooperative study.

Undertake cooperative planning for continuing education
programs for library personnel within the western region
under the auspices of the Commission.

Stimulate research in librarianship with colleges and universities and other appropriate groups.

Adopt and recommend budgets to implement the above.

Programs of the Council shall not, however, inhibit or inter-
fere with programs sponsored by individual members of the
Council.

II - FUNDING

The programs of the Council shall be funded by the member

states and by gifts, grants, and contracts in a manner to be
determined by the members of the Council.

III - MEMBERSHIP

Section 1. Eligibility.
Membership in the Council shall be open to state library
agencies located in the states which are parties to the
Western Regional Education Compact.

Section 2. Representation.
Representatives to the Council shall be named by the State
Librarian of each library participating in the program;
the representative need not be a staff member of the
library.

Section 3. Withdrawal.
Members may withdraw from the Council by giving six
months notice of intent.

IV - MEETINGS

Section 1. Meetings.
The Council shall meet at such intervals and at such places
as may be required to conduct its business. Meetings shall
be held upon the call of the Chairman, upon the written request of three members, or at the request of the Commission. The first meeting of the fiscal year shall be desig-
nated as the Annual Meeting of the Council. Expenses of
representatives attending Council meetings shall be borne by
the Council.

Section 2. Voting.
Each official representative of a state library agency
holding membership in the Council shall be entitled to
one vote.

V - OFFICERS, TERMS, DUTIES

Section 1. Council Officers.
The officers of the Council shall be a chairman and a vice-
chairman. The officers shall be elected at the Annual Meeting of the Council.

Section 2. Terms.
The term of office shall be for one year or until successors
have been elected or appointed and qualified.

Section 3. Duties.
The officers shall perform the usual duties of their respec-
tive offices, including the following:

   (a) Chairman. The chairman of the Council shall: pre-
        pare agenda for the meetings; appoint committees;
        represent the Council in the intervals between its
        meetings; report at the next following meeting of
        each body all action taken in its behalf.

   (b) Vice-chairman. The vice-chairman of the Council
        shall: perform all duties of the chairman of the
        Council in the absence of the chairman.

VI - COMMITTEES

Section 1. Committees.
The council may at any meeting authorize the creation of
such committees as it deems necessary and appropriate, and
may fix their size, duties and tenure.

VII - PROFESSIONAL STAFF

Section 1. Professional Staff.
The Council shall have the services of a professional staff
whose members shall be on the staff of the Commission and
shall serve as administrator of Council programs.

Section 2. Functions.
The professional staff shall provide secretarial services and
coordinate the work of the Council.

VIII - DISSOLUTION

The Council may be dissolved by vote of three-fourths of the
funding members.

IX - ADOPTION OF CHARTER

This Charter shall become effective upon the assent of the
state library agencies whose representatives' signatures appear below. In giving its assent, each library recognizes
that it has committed itself to work with the other parties to
the Charter in developing continuing education programs for
library personnel.

IN WITNESS WHEREOF each party to this Charter has affixed
its seal and signature on the date indicated.

ESEA TITLE II CONTRIBUTIONS
TO STATE DEPARTMENT OF EDUCATION
LEADERSHIP OF SCHOOL MEDIA PROGRAMS

Milbrey L. Jones

> The history of school libraries shows that the
> state education and library agencies have had key
> roles in the establishment and improvement of
> school libraries. Much of the work has been
> carried on through the state office of school li-
> brary supervision, and it is generally true on a
> statewide basis that school libraries have reached
> a higher state of development in those states that
> have had school library supervision.[1]

Although there are many events which have contributed
to the development of school library/media programs within
State departments of education, one of the most significant in
the last decade has been Title II of the Elementary and Secondary Education Act. This paper analyzes Title II contributions to State department of education leadership in school
media program development in terms of seven management
functions: supervision and leadership; planning State school
media programs; coordination and cooperation; certification
of school media specialists; school media standards; statistics, evaluation, and research; and budgeting and finance.[2]

Supervision and Leadership

The thrust toward provision of leadership to plan and
effect improvements in State school library/media programs
began well before enactment of Title II. The first State
school library supervisory position was established in Wisconsin in 1891.[3] Other States followed in establishing similar positions until by 1959, there were 34 professional

70

school library consultants in 23 State departments of education.[4] Renewed interest in State school library supervision
developed in the early 1960s as a result of three publications
which shaped public understanding of the role of State departments of education in school library development.

Standards for School Library Programs outlined
the duties of chief State school officers and State
school library consultants with respect to school
libraries.[5]

State Department of Education Responsibilities for
School Libraries analyzed the status of State services for school libraries.[6]

Responsibilities of State Departments of Education
for School Library Services was a policy statement
issued by the Council of Chief State School Officers
based on the above study.[7]

Between 1960 and 1965, State school library supervision steadily advanced, influenced strongly by the 1960
school library standards and by the grants financed in a number of States by the School Library Development Project of
the American Association of School Librarians.[8] The latter
involved extensive campaigns to interpret the significance of
school libraries and the role of standards in improving them.

A further advance toward the goal of at least one
State school library supervisor in every State was provided
by Title II of the Elementary and Secondary Education Act.
Signed into law in April 1965, Title II provided, for the first
time, direct Federal financial assistance for the acquisition
of school library resources, textbooks, and other instructional materials for the use of children and teachers in public and private elementary and secondary schools. The program consists of two basic components--acquisition and
administration.

The acquisition program includes the purchase, lease-
purchase, or straight lease of school library resources,
textbooks, and other instructional materials. Administration
includes the executive, supervisory, and management responsibilities necessary to carry out State plans. Title II allows
five per cent of the amount paid to the State, or $50,000,
whichever is greater, for administration of the program.

The amounts reported for State administration of Title II during the first eight years represented 4.1 per cent of the amount expended, somewhat less then the sum actually available (Table 1). These figures reflect the tendency of States to make sparing use of funds for administration, choosing instead to devote funds as much as possible to acquisition of materials for use in instructional programs. The major part of ESEA Title II administrative funds went into salaries of administrators, supervisors, and clerical personnel assigned to the program.

The actual materials made available under Title II constituted an important contribution to education; however, the leadership provided through the program is also significant. Several States, with low populations and rural areas, particularly in the West and New England, were able, under Title II, to employ State school library supervisors for the first time. At one point in 1969, there were about 120 State school library consultants in 48 States and the District of Columbia.[9] There are now about 83 State school library consultants in 37 States and the District of Columbia. The decline over the past three years reflects the decrease in Title II allotments and the financial strictures of State departments of education.

The administrative funds provided under Title II helped establish sound programs of staff development for local school personnel participating in Title II. In-service education activities were designed to help teachers and media specialists understand the value of a broad base of media, become familiar with materials, and use them effectively. Examples of staff development opportunities offered through the program are:

> Development of multimedia presentations on Title II describing for school personnel and lay groups the use of media in instructional programs;

> Utilization in Massachusetts of Title II funds to sponsor a workshop, "The Urban Child--Extending the Right to Read." Special attention was given to the learning needs of black and Spanish-speaking children;

> Two conferences for school media leadership in California to influence the immediate and long-range developments of school media programs

Table 1. Funds available and funds expended for State administration and for acquisitions under ESEA title II programs: Fiscal years 1966-73

Fiscal year	Allotment	Expenditures						Total Expenditures (cols. 3+5) (plus Percent of Allotment Expended)	
		Administration		Acquisitions					
		Amount	Percent	Amount	Percent				
(1)	(2)	(3)	(4)	(5)	(6)			(7)	(8)
1966.........	$100,000,000	$ 2,049,362	2.1	$ 95,298,079	98.0			$ 97,347,441	97.3
1967.........	102,000,000	3,885,118	3.8	95,745,032	96.2			99,627,150	97.6
1968.........	99,234,000	4,427,912	4.4	94,024,821	95.5			98,452,733	99.2
1969.........	50,000,000	3,047,522	6.1	46,153,184	93.8			49,200,706	98.4
1970.........	42,500,000	2,431,133	6.5	34,913,640	93.6			37,344,733	87.8*
1971.........	80,000,000	3,281,932	4.7	67,343,321	95.3			70,625,253	88.2*
1972.........	90,000,000	3,217,932	4.0	76,260,690	95.1			79,477,964	88.3*
1973**......	100,000,000	3,360,000	4.0	80,640,000	96.0			84,000,000	84.0***
Total........	663,734,000	25,700,253	4.1	590,378,767	95.9			616,790,000	92.9

*A statutory amendment permitted carryover to the next year of unexpended funds.

**Estimated

***Of the amount appropriated in fiscal year 1973, only $90 million was released in that year. The remaining $10 million was realeased in fiscal year 1974.

and plan better utilization of media, media personnel,
and services. Authorities in several disciplines and
professions helped participants examine current
problems.

Planning State School Media Programs

Suggestions appropriate to the planning function for State
school media programs are:

Development of a long-range plan for providing
leadership and services;

Periodic review of the plan in the light of accom-
plishments, goals, new trends, and research
findings;

Assurance of plan implementation through provision
of continuous cooperation of staff members.

Prior to 1965, there was considerable planning activity in State departments of education in relation to school
library media programs, particularly in States with longer
histories of school library supervision. Evidence of implementation of plans is apparent in the early establishment of
elementary school libraries, revision and formulation of
standards, and State aid for school libraries.

Planning for ESEA Title II was frequently fitted skill-
fully into the full range of State school media activity; however, it was affected somewhat by the varied patterns of organization in State departments of education for Title II administration. Program administration is variously located
in Divisions of Instruction, Federal-State Divisions, or other
units. In some instances, Title II administrative funds and
the increased media services provided by State department of
education personnel stimulated organization of comprehensive
educational media programs into a single unit. In State
agencies where unified school media administrative organization has not been achieved, patterns of cooperative planning
among concerned units help achieve coordinated services.

One State department of education, now in its eighth
year of implementation of a coordinated school media program,
has a Division of Educational Media. Division responsibilities include leadership of unified media programs, Federal

programs for instructional media, television education, and textbooks. Professional staff assist county and city school administrative units to establish and extend media services, including school television programs of instruction.

In 1971, State departments of education developed new plans for Title II administration. These plans stimulated use of a management by objectives system which required needs assessment, development of goals and objectives, formulation of a performance plan, and evaluation. Such plans are in use in many States and are assisting in charting a course toward achieving Title II objectives as well as overall State objectives for school media programs.

Many State school media specialists are now involved in State-wide planning for education including plans for State, regional, and local media programs as a component. Additional momentum was given in 1970-72 to State leadership in planning and evaluation by Title IV, Section 402, P. L. 90-247. Long-range planning in State departments of education appears to be moving in the direction of cost effectiveness studies and planning-programming-budgeting systems.

Coordination and Cooperation

The sub-functions of State departments of education which apply to coordination and cooperation in school media programs are cooperation with governmental and non-governmental agencies and internal cooperation with other related departmental programs concerned with media services.

The Federal-State partnership in Title II administration began when representatives of State departments of education and the U. S. Office of Education became involved in conferences prior to approval of State plans. The purposes of these conferences were to ascertain needs, design effective methods of administration, and arrive at general acceptance and understanding of the program. The plans have worked smoothly and agreeable relationships between State departments of education and the U. S. Office of Education have been maintained.

State-Federal cooperation in education has been enhanced under Title II through U. S. Office of Education sponsorship of various types of regional and national conferences. One purpose of these conferences has been to obtain from

State personnel suggestions for improving the program. The
conferences, attended by Title II coordinators, media and
reading supervisors, and other State personnel, have dealt
with various phases of program management such as planning,
evaluation, and dissemination. They have provided opportunity for information exchange and offered presentations concerned with media services to disadvantaged children living
in urban and isolated areas.

Periodic reviews of Title II administration have provided additional opportunities for State and Federal personnel
to cooperate in improving media services. Continual communication with State Title II personnel is maintained through
program memoranda, telephone contact, correspondence related to program administration, and publications. State department of education personnel have cooperated in the evaluation of Title II by assisting in determining the areas,
methods, and objectives of evaluation, as well as in the
actual work. [11]

The chief influence of Title II on State department of
education cooperation with non-governmental agencies has
been relationships which have developed with private school
officials. Title II provides that, to the extent consistent
with State law, school library resources, textbooks, and
other instructional materials acquired under the program are
to be provided on an equitable basis for the use of children
and teachers in private elementary and secondary schools in
the State which comply with compulsory attendance laws or
are otherwise recognized through some other procedure cus-
tomarily used. State department of education personnel, local public school administrators, and private school authorities report favorably on the relationship between public and
private school officials in connection with the program. Representatives of private schools serve on Title II advisory
committees and have been useful in developing acceptance
and understanding of the program.

The administration of Title II facilitates internal coordination of State media activity with other department programs. Subject area consultants and other staff assist in
the preparation of Title II State plans, program guidelines,
and forms; review Title II project applications; assist in
selection of materials; and monitor projects. In turn,
Title II administrators and supervisors perform similar services for other programs and provide technical assistance in
media services. Title II personnel have also worked with

local Federal coordinators, school administrators, media
staff, and teachers through personal contacts, workshops,
conferences, and onsite visits to assist in the best use of
State, Federal, and local funds for media services.

Certification of School Media Specialists

Although Title II impact on activity in the certification
of media personnel has been indirect, most States credit the
program with stimulating awareness of the need for additional
and better trained personnel. Reports from State departments
of education indicate the employment of significant numbers
of school media personnel:

> The number of school district central offices re-
> porting employment of media specialists rose from
> 5,850 in 1964-65 to 8,469 in 1967-68, about 20 per
> cent appointed as a result of Title II;

> The number of school district central offices with
> media aides increased by 59 per cent between 1964-
> 65 and 1967-68, with 38 per cent reporting that
> Title II was primarily responsible;

> Of 8,495 adding at least one media specialist over
> a three-year period, 41 per cent reported that
> Title II was primarily responsible. [12]

The increased staff in school media centers and the
new and complex demands placed on them have created renewed interest in certification. Media specialists are assuming new teaching responsibilities and receive mounting
requests for their time and services as specialists in the
selection and use of media. The instructional needs of
schools which require media specialists with education in
the general media field plus specialization--by educational
level, subject matter, or type of media--is a further com-
plication.

Spurred by these new developments, many States are
studying and refining media certification requirements. State
school media consultants assist in formulating and revising
new certification requirements. In Maine, for example, com-
petency-based certification for library/media specialists was
developed by committees composed of State department of
education staff, representatives from colleges and universities,

the Maine School Library Association, and the Maine Audiovisual Association.   In reporting on Title II impact, States
call attention to the increasing awareness of the need to reassess and reorganize staffing patterns.   In New York, as
in other States, State education agency personnel have ad-
dressed the task of determining appropriate and effective
roles for paraprofessionals, teachers, technicians, aides,
and media specialists in provision of media services.

Standards for School Media Programs

      One of the functions State departments of education
fulfill in Title II administration is development, revision,
dissemination, and evaluation of standards relating to the
selection, acquisition, and use of school library resources,
textbooks, and other instructional materials.   The purpose
of standards in the program is to establish new or revised
levels for the materials obtained.   They serve the general
purpose of all educational standards--to set minimum levels
below which no instructional program can be effective, and
stimulate efforts to surpass standards and move toward ex-
cellence in educational quality and opportunity.

      A U. S. Office of Education survey reported in 1964
that only three States--Alaska, Massachusetts, and Utah--
and the Virgin Islands did not have State school library standards;   however, the standards of five other States--Alabama,
Maine, New Hampshire, Vermont, and West Virginia--were
for secondary schools only. [13]   Since 1964, the 50 States, the
District of Columbia, Guam, Puerto Rico, the Virgin Islands,
the Trust Territory of the Pacific Islands, and the Bureau
of Indian Affairs have either developed or revised standards
for school library resources in elementary and secondary
schools for use in the Title II program, or have adopted the
official standards of a professional organization.   Administrative funds from Title II have assisted State departments
of education to evaluate and revise standards and disseminate
and interpret them through publications, conferences, workshops, and other program activities.

      Standards are used in the Title II program to ascer-
tain the need of elementary and secondary school children
for learning resources and establish formulas for the distribution of materials.   The activity in relation to standards
was encouraged by the 1969 school media standards[14] and
by widespread recognition that State standards are often

inadequate quantitatively and insufficient in scope to meet contemporary instructional program demands. In addition to the need for increased quantities of printed and audiovisual media, extended use of technology, newer teaching methods, and recognition of the specialized competencies needed by media personnel are important influences in school media standard revision and formulation.

State, regional, and national standards have changed rapidly since the inception of Title II. A preliminary survey of standards presently used under the Title II program indicates several trends:

> The 1969 standards of the American Association of School Librarians and the Department of Audiovisual Instruction (now called the Association for Education Communications and Technology) have influenced State standards[14] and the cooperation of these organizations has stimulated similar cooperation between State organizations;

> State standards tend to emulate national standards in provisions to facilitate a unified approach to media services;

> There appears to be an increasing tendency to include recommendations for school district media services;

> Standards are being developed in phases or levels;

> All States and areas with standards have standards for elementary schools.[15]

Statistics, Research, and Evaluation

Federal requirements pertaining to management of the Title II program have influenced the collection, analysis, and dissemination of statistics and other pertinent evaluative information on the scope and quality of school media services. One of the major requirements of the program is the distribution of school library resources, textbooks, and other instructional materials among eligible children and teachers according to relative need.   Criteria for relative need are established based on a comparative analysis and the application of standards.   Data needed to establish relative need are obtained from surveys of schools and school systems on media available to children and teachers.

Criteria applied in deciding relative need are reviewed from time to time and adjusted to changing needs. This continuing revision of relative need formulas has required State departments of education to conduct periodic surveys of media collections in schools. Although many States have for years collected different information on library/media programs, several used Title II funds to assist in developing a more coordinated system for collecting statistics. Kentucky, Maryland, Missouri, New Jersey, Oregon, and Wisconsin are among States which have produced valuable statistics on school media programs for administrative reports, reports to the U.S. Office of Education, and for use by schools in support of local programs.

Such reports provide information on the quantity and quality of materials provided by Federal, State, and local effort and the effect of increased materials on program, staff, and facilities. For example, in 1970 New York launched a comprehensive survey of all aspects of the school media program including holdings of all media, equipment, facilities, personnel, administrative practices, budget, etc. The survey included regional media centers and school district services, as well as individual schools.

In some instances, media personnel in State departments of education have become involved in more complex types of evaluation such as impact of media services on elementary and secondary school teaching and learning.[16] Observations of model programs and case studies indicate extensive increase in pupil and teacher use of newer media and some evidences of change from textbook-oriented teaching to use of a broad range of media. Several States are considering broadening research and evaluation services by initiating projects to determine teacher and pupil needs for media services and formulating objective criteria for evaluating programs. In some cases, these plans are part of an overall State-wide educational planning and evaluation capability.

Media personnel in State departments of education have also assisted graduate students with studies of Title II impact:

Billings, R. G. Study to Evaluate the Effect of

the Minnesota Plan (ESEA Title II) on the Development of Selected School Libraries. Unpublished paper, Western Michigan University, 1969.

Graham, Robert James. The Impact of Title II of the Elementary and Secondary Education Act on Selected Michigan High Schools. Unpublished doctoral dissertation, University of Michigan, Ann Arbor, 1969.

May, Frank Curtis. The California School Library Program Funded Through the Elementary and Secondary Education Act, Title II, Phase II, for 1965-66. Unpublished doctoral dissertation, University of Denver, 1971.

Morris, Jacqueline G. The Demonstration School Libraries Project in North Carolina, 1966-67. Unpublished master's essay, Wayne State University, Detroit, 1967.

Tyler, Ellen. A Study of the Utilization of an Elementary and Secondary Education Act, Title II, Phase II, Instructional Materials Center in an Elementary School. Unpublished paper, San Diego State College, 1969.

Ward, Pearl Lewis. Federal Aid to School Libraries: A Study of the Phase II, Title II Program in California, 1965-66. Unpublished doctoral dissertation, University of Southern California, Los Angeles, 1967.

Budgeting and Finance

Activities related to the budgeting and finance of State school media programs include making periodic appraisals of program needs and translating them into financial requirements. Additional areas of responsibility include requesting funds sufficient for State services in the department budget, inclusion of media personnel and materials in the State's plan for financial aid to local school units, and maintenance of standards requiring sufficient financial support for school media programs.

The percentages of total budgets for State department

of education media services that are represented by Title II
administrative funds are not available. Since, however, in
several States, the only school media/library consultant employed either serves as Title II coordinator or is assigned
to the program for a large portion of his time, it may be
assumed that in those States, Title II administrative funds
represent a fair contribution to the support of State media
services.

At least once a year, Title II administrative supervisory and supervisory staff in State departments of education are required to examine administrative and program
practices to evaluate their effectiveness and determine what
changes are needed. These reviews have been helpful in
Statewide appraisal of all media program needs and determination of financial resources required for media personnel,
equipment, materials, and facilities. This information has
proved useful in several States for justifying increased departmental budgets and additional State aid for regional and
local school media services.

The preliminary survey of the newer school media
standards revised or formulated for use in the Title II program reveals that standards for school media expenditures
are being increased. The Title II maintenance of effort requirement has had some influence in stimulating recommendations for higher levels of support. [17] It should be noted
that these increases are insufficient to compensate for the
rise in cost of media and media services. Also, some standards include recommendations for unified media programs
without recommending funds and staff to support them.

There are at least three States--Delaware, Idaho, and
Maryland--which outline State responsibility for library/me-
dia services in their standards. Such interpretation of the
role of State departments of education in media activity is
an important step toward obtaining the financial support necessary for State services.

Conclusion

Title II of the Elementary and Secondary Education
Act has, as its basic purpose, provision of increased quantities of high quality media for the use of children and
teachers in public and private elementary and secondary
schools. The related services provided through State

administration of the program have also directly and indirectly
provided State departments of education with opportunities to
strengthen services for school media programs by:

Adding school media consultant positions and aug-
menting leadership activities;

Motivating improved educational planning and management of State media services;

Encouraging cooperative efforts in many areas for
coordination of school media programs;

Stimulating awareness of the more specialized competencies needed by school media personnel;

Promoting revision, formulation, or adoption of
school media standards;

Contributing to the improvement of school media
statistical, research, and evaluation services;

Exerting direct influence on the assessment of
State school media services and determination of
financial needs to implement programs.

The changes in State school library/media supervision
since the 1960 study, State Department of Education Responsibilities for School Libraries, are substantial. It is evident
that State school media services could become a vital part
of State educational leadership services. More complete information is needed on the current status of State media services as measures of change and growth since 1960 and to
determine more precisely the influence of Federal programs.

State and Federal efforts to fund State department of
education media services continue, however, to fall short of
being adequate. Staffing and services in a number of States
are at lower levels than in the early years of Title II. Even
in those years, administrative funds from Title II were insufficient to obtain the personnel needed. The goal proposed in
1960 of at least one State school library supervisor for every
State has not been met.[18] State leadership for school media
programs can be effective only when there is in every State
a comprehensive and coordinated media program, adequately
staffed and funded, and given the full support of State school
officials.

Notes

1. American Association of School Librarians. Standards
    for School Library Programs. Chicago, American
    Library Association, 1960, p. 30.

2. Council of Chief State School Officers. Responsibilities
    of State Departments of Education for School Library
    Services. Washington, D. C., Council of Chief State
    School Officers, 1961, p. 8.

3. Mary Helen Mahar. State Department of Education Re-
    sponsibilities for School Libraries. Washington,
    D. C., U. S. Department of Health, Education, and
    Welfare, Office of Education, p. 9.

4. Ibid., p. 10.

5. American Association of School Librarians, op. cit.

6. Mahar, op. cit.

7. Council of Chief State School Officers, op. cit.

8. Mary Francis Kennon and Leila Doyle. Planning School
    Library Development; a Report of the School Library
    Development Project, American Association of School
    Librarians, February 1, 1961-July 31, 1952. Chi-
    cago, American Library Association, 1962.

9. Milbrey L. Jones. "School Media Programs: Progress,
    Obstacles, and Promising Developments," in Mary Vir-
    ginia Gaver, ed., State-Wide Library Planning: The
    New Jersey Example. New Brunswick, New Jersey,
    Rutgers University Press, 1964, pp. 45-62.

10. These data are estimates based on a mimeographed list
    issued by the U. S. Office of Education.

11. Mary Helen Mahar. "Evaluation of Media Services to
    Children and Young People in Schools," Library
    Trends 22:377-86, 1974.

12. An Evaluative Survey Report on ESEA Title II: Fiscal
    Years 1966-68, Part I: Analysis and Interpretation.
    Washington, D. C., U. S. Department of Health, Edu-
    cation, and Welfare, Office of Education, 1972,
    pp. 49-57.

13. Richard L. Darling. Survey of School Library Stan-
     dards. Washington, D. C. , U. S. Department of
     Health, Education, and Welfare, Office of Education,
     1964, pp. 4-5.

14. American Association of School Librarians and Depart-
     ment of Audiovisual Instruction. Standards for
     School Media Programs. Chicago and Washington,
     D. C. , American Library Association and National
     Education Association, 1969.

15. These data are based on a survey of school media stan-
     dards now being completed at the U. S. Office of
     Education.

16. U. S. Department of Health, Education, and Welfare,
     Education Division, Office of Education. Annual
     Report, Fiscal Year 1972, Title II, Elementary and
     Secondary Education Act, P. L. 89-10, As Amended,
     School Library Resources, Textbooks, and Other
     Instructional Materials. Washington, D. C. , U. S.
     Government Printing Office, 1973, pp. 31-48.

17. An Evaluative Survey Report on ESEA Title II: Fiscal
     Years 1966-68, op. cit. , p. 75.

18. American Association of School Librarians, op. cit. ,
     p. 26.

PART III

SCIENTIFIC MANAGEMENT
AND STATISTICS

COMPOUND GROWTH IN LIBRARIES

Fred Heinritz

> A library will grow and grow
> Despite its shrinking storage space.
> Through summer sun, through winter snow
> A library will grow and grow
> (Though when mature its rate may slow).
> However fast or slow the pace
> A library will grow and grow
> Despite its shrinking storage space.

Mathematical Models

The concept of seeking out and utilizing abstract mathematical models that correspond to actual occurrences in the natural world has been with us for many centuries. As early as 1609 Kepler published his first law of planetary motion. This law states that the planets move round the sun in ellipses, the sun being one of the foci. This is equivalent to saying that the orbit of a planet obeys the equation for an ellipse, with the sun understood to be at one focus.

We need not worry here about understanding the mathematical details. The crucial point is that the ellipse, a form of conic section that had been studied as an abstract intellectual exercise by the Greeks many centuries before, was found to describe an important phenomenon in the real world--the orbits of planets. An important result of this correspondence is that it is now possible to predict the orbit of a planet accurately in advance, on theoretical grounds alone. Books of tables such as the American Ephemeris and Nautical Almanac are prepared in this manner, by computers utilizing the proper equations.

The use of mathematical models in the social sciences

is a more recent development. Here the correspondence between model and phenomenon is less exact than in the physical sciences. Nonetheless usefully close correspondence
with models is widely observable. Library science is no
exception.

Library Growth Models

"The library is a growing organism," states Ranganathan's fifth Law of Library Science. It has been that way
for a long time. According to Sarton "... the Library [of
Alexandria] grew very rapidly. The original building was
already too small by the middle of the third century [B.C.],
and it was necessary to create a secondary library in the
Sarapeion."[1]

One of the most pervasive characteristics of libraries
is their inexorable tendency to grow. Empirical evidence
indicates that until they become extremely large, American
academic and research libraries grow at a rate of about 4
or 5 per cent annually, which doubles their size in about
sixteen or seventeen years.[2] Smaller libraries often grow
considerably faster. To help plan for and contend with this
fact a mathematical model of growth (in number of books
acquired, card drawers, etc.) would seem to be a useful
predictive tool for librarians.

Various growth models can be applied to library problems. We shall confine our discussion to a single one of
wide application--the model for a constant rate of growth.
Although this model, like all mathematical models, is abstract and can pertain to any field, its best known application has been in the area of business and finance. For this
reason, it will be introduced in this context. The implications for libraries will then be drawn.

Simple Interest

Simple interest is paid only on the original principal,
and not on the interest accrued. It may be expressed by
the formula:

$$I = Pin \tag{1}$$

where   I = Simple interest

P = Original principal
i = Annual rate of interest
n = Number of years during which interest is paid.

If one starts with P dollars and earns simple interest at rate i on this money for n years, he will end up with an amount equal to original principal plus interest:

$$A = P + Pin$$
$$A = P(1 + in)$$

(2)

where   A = The amount of money at the end of n years.

Thus if we start with a principal of $100,000 earning 6 per cent annually, the amounts at the end of each of the first three years would be:

1st Year $A = P(1 + in) = \$100,000 (1 + (.06)1) = \$106,000$
2nd Year $A = P(1 + 2i) = \$100,000 (1 + (.06)2) = \$112,000$
3rd Year $A = P(1 + 3i) = \$100,000 (1 + (.06)3) = \$118,000$

Such a model describes a constant number of units (in this case iP dollars) added per year. A constant number of units added per year results in a decreasing rate of growth. This is easily seen from the above equations. By definition the rate of growth is:

Rate of Growth = Interest Earned During Year x
for Year x   Amount at End of Year (x - 1)

Thus the rate of growth for each of the first three years is:

1st Year   iP/ P   = i
2nd Year   iP/ (P + iP)   = i/ (1 + i)
3rd Year   iP/ (P + 2iP)   = i/ (1 + 2i)

Clearly the growth rate decreases with time.

Compound Interest

Compound interest refers to interest computed on the accumulated unpaid interest as well as on the original principal. If we start with an original principal of P earning an annual rate of interest i, then the amount A at the end of the first year is:

$$A = P + iP = P (1 + i)$$

For the second year, interest is earned not on P alone, but on P (1 + i), the amount at the end of the first year, giving an amount:

$$A = P (1 + i) + P (1 + i) i$$
$$A = P (1 + i) (1 + i) = P (1 + i)^2$$

Continuing in this manner, it is easy to see that the general formula is:

$$A = P (1 + i)^n \qquad (3)$$

where   n = Number of years during which interest is paid.

With original principal P of \$100,000 and annual rate of interest i the amounts at the end of each of the first three years would be:

1st Year $A = P (1 + i)$ = \$100,000 (1.06)   = \$106,000
2nd Year $A = P (1 + i)^2$ = \$100,000 (1.06)^2 = \$112,360
3rd Year $A = P (1 + i)^3$ = \$100,000 (1.06)^3 = \$119,101

Comparing these formulas and computations with those for simple interest brings out several important points. In compound interest the rate of growth is constant:

1st Year   iP/ P   = i
2nd Year   iP (1 + i) / P (1 + i)   = i
3rd Year   iP (1 + i)^2 / P (1 + i)^2 = i

However, the number of dollars added increases each successive year. Thus the amount at the end of the second and third years is greater with compound than with simple interest. This difference is not of substantial magnitude for the first few years, but increases with time. The greater the rate of interest, the greater the difference. If for any given original principal and rate of interest we plot amount against time on Cartesian coordinates, the locus of points for an amount earning simple interest is a straight line, and for an amount earning compound interest a positive exponential curve. If we plot both models on the same graph using identical initial values, the two lines will be seen to diverge widely as the number of years increases.

The $(1 + i)^n$ term in the compound interest formula becomes difficult to compute by hand for large n. Fortunately, because compound interest calculations are used so

widely in business, many tables are available solving the
amount formula (3) with unit original principal for various
rates and years.[3] For a given case we multiply the appropriate table value by the specific principal of the problem to
determine the amount. Figure 1 is such a table. For i =
6% and n = 3, the table value is 1.19. For P = $100,000,
this gives an amount of

$$A = \$100,000 \ (1.19) = \$119,000$$

which is (within rounding errors) the same result obtained a
few paragraphs above.

The Future Size of Collection and Catalog

It was stated in Section 2 that the constant rate of
growth model is an appropriate one to describe the growth
of most library collections. The librarian is courting
trouble to predict future space needs by extrapolating on the
basis of the number of current acquisitions--i.e., by using
the simple interest model. For example, from Figure 1 we
see that the expression $(1.06)^{10}$ has a value of 1.79. The
corresponding expression for a constant number of units
added, $(1 + (.06)10)$, is 1.60. The ratio 1.60/1.79 being
only 0.89, it is easy to see that a ten-year estimate based
on the wrong model would fall about 11 per cent short of
true need.

For library collections the original principal P refers
to the current number of books in the collection. The
amount refers to the size of the collection at n years in the
future if it grows at annual rate i. Thus if a library currently has 500,000 volumes, and a 6 per cent growth rate,
in ten years the collection will have grown to 895,000
volumes:

$$A = 500,000 \ (1.06)^{10}$$
$$A = 500,000 \ (1.79)$$
$$A = 895,000$$

In the same way, if a library catalog contains 500,000 cards
(or a book catalog 500,000 entries), with i = 6 per cent, its
size in ten years would be about 895,000 cards (or entries).

Additional Shelving or Catalog Drawers Needed

The number of volumes or cards added during the next n years will be (A - P). If all shelving units or catalog drawers, present and to be, are the same size, then the formula

$$A - P = P (1 + i)^n - P$$
$$A - P = P [(1 + i)^n - 1] \qquad (4)$$

can be used to determine the number of additional shelving units or card drawers which must be purchased for an expansion to last a given number of years. Thus if we desire a catalog expansion to last five years beyond present capacity, if the annual catalog growth rate is 7 per cent, and if the present number of drawers is 540, 216 additional drawers are required:

$$A - P = 540 [(1.07)^5 - 1]$$
$$A - P = 540 (.40)$$
$$A - P = 216$$

Predicting Time Remaining Before More Shelving Units or Catalog Drawers Are Required

It is also important to be able to determine the amount of time remaining before shelving space runs out, and more is required. To do this it is necessary to solve the compound interest formula for n:

$$A = P (1 + i)^n$$
$$\log (A/P) = n \log (1 + i) \qquad (5)$$
$$n = \log (A/P)/\log (1 + i)$$

Because of book shifting problems, the practical working capacity of shelving (the amount A) is less than 100 per cent. (Metcalf suggests 86 per cent).[4] Clearly A and P can be expressed either in terms of numbers of volumes or of percentage of working capacity.

If a library has a working capacity of 240,000 volumes, a present size of 178,000 volumes and a growth rate of 6 per cent, it will need additional shelving in just over five years:

$$n = \log (240,000/178,000)/\log (1.06)$$
$$n = \log (1.35)/\log (1.06)$$
$$n = 0.1303/0.0253$$
$$n = 5.2$$

Manual solution of equation (5) is a nuisance. The same approximate result can be obtained from Figure 1. Scan down the appropriate rate column until you come to the value most closely approximating the value of the ratio (A/P) for the given data. This row indicates the years remaining until more shelving is required. Interpolate for additional accuracy if it is desired. Thus for the above problem the (A/P) ratio is 1.35. Looking down the 6 per cent column we find the value 1.34, indicating a time of just over five years.

A more convenient table, giving the desired times directly is printed as Figure 2. The fact that the table headings are in terms of card catalogs is immaterial, and simply shows that the same formula applies to them as well as book collections.[5] Note that the Figure 2 answer to the above problem is 5.2 years.

All techniques discussed so far are as applicable to book as to card catalogs. Suppose a book catalog growing at 6 per cent annually is cumulated at each 100,000 entries. There are 80,000 entries currently in the supplements to be cumulated. This gives an (A/P) ratio of 1.25. Figure 2 tells us it will be about 3.8 years until the next cumulation will be required.

Special Storage for Less-Used Materials

Empirical evidence[6] indicates that the average circulation of library materials decreases with time expired since their acquisition or publication. Because of this phenomenon some large libraries which are hard-pressed for storage space separate the collection on the basis of age of acquisition, putting the older items into a special storage area for less-used materials. Such an area may be in another part of town where land costs are less, and may be especially planned for compact storage, to utilize space to the maximum.

To determine such a cut-off point rationally, the library administrator needs to know the approximate proportion

of his library's collection that should go to special storage
for any given cut-off year, and the amount of circulation
from special storage that this would entail. The first problem is considered in this section; the proportion of circulation in the next.

If the library acquisition rate is approximately constant, the proportion in special storage is easy to determine.
If the beginning year of the collection was t years ago, and
we desire to relocate all books acquired more than n years
ago, as shown in Figure 3, then the proportion in special
storage (propspec) is:

Propspec = $\dfrac{\text{Books Acquired More Than n Years Ago}}{\text{Total Size of Collection}}$

Propspec = $P (1 + i)^{t-n}/P (1 + i)^{t}$

Propspec = $(1 + i)^{-n}$

Propspec = $1/(1 + i)^{n}$

(6)

This expression, $1/(1 + i)^{n}$, is well known to the
business world as the present value for unit amount, and is
obtained by solving the compound interest equation (3) with
A set equal to one:

$1 = P (1 + i)^{n}$

$P = 1/(1 + i)^{n}$

Because of its importance in business, present value tables
are widely available. [7] Figure 4 is such a table. From it
we may read directly the proportion in special storage.
Thus if we relocate all books acquired more than ten years
ago, and i is 6 per cent, 0.56 or 56 per cent of the collection would go into special storage.

Proportion of Circulation from Special Storage

In addition to knowing the proportion of the collection
to go into special storage for a given cut-off date, the library planner needs to know the approximate proportion of
the total circulation which is due to the stored items. To
determine this, it is necessary to utilize the concept of negative growth. Existing evidence indicates that the average

circulation of library materials decreases at a fairly steady
rate as the time elapsed since their publication or acquisition
increases. [8] We shall call this annual obsolescence rate d.
If we again define the start of the collection as t years ago,
and we desire to relocate all books acquired more than n
years ago, the proportion of circulation from special storage
(propcirc) is:

Propcirc = Annual Circulation of Books Acquired More
                Than n Years Ago/Total Annual Circulation

$$\text{Propcirc} = \frac{1-d}{1+i}^{\,n} \tag{7}$$

This formula, developed from basic growth model equations
by Leimkuhler, [9] is derived in the Appendix.

    Figure 5 gives solutions for a variety of cut-off dates,
given a specific growth rate (6 per cent) and obsolescence
rate (5 per cent). It may be seen that the proportion of
circulation from storage is always less than the proportion
of the collection in storage, and that the disparity increases
as the cut-off year is pushed back in time.

    Figures 6 and 7 used together allow the computation
of the proportion of circulation from storage for growth and
obsolescence rates ranging from 3 to 12 per cent. Figure 6
gives the value of $(1 - d)/(1 + i)$, and Figure 7 raises this
result to the (n)th power, to give Propcirc. Thus if i = 6
per cent, d = 5 per cent, and n = 10, Figure 6 indicates
that $(1 - d)/(1 + i)$ has a value of 0.896. Carrying this
result to Figure 7 and using simple interpolation, we get:

Propcirc = 0.312 + (0.006/(0.905 - 0.890)) (0.369 - 0.312)

Propcirc = 0.312 + (0.4) (0.057)

Propcirc = 0.33

This agrees with the result for n = 10 given in Figure 5.

Conclusion

    There seems little doubt of the pragmatic potential of
the preceding material. In addition to its utilitarian aspect,
some of it, such as the formula for the proportion of

circulation from special storage, is in itself of considerable intellectual interest. Most important of all, however, is the fact that other mathematical models apply equally well to other areas of library management. The literature in this area is increasing rapidly (perhaps at a constant growth rate?). To encourage wider dissemination, acceptance and use of this work it is hoped that mathematical specialists writing in the area of library management will take greater cognizance than heretofore that librarians cannot profit from literature that their training does not enable them to understand; and that librarians will make more effort than so far exhibited to upgrade their level of numerical proficiency.

Notes

1. George Sarton. A History of Science; Hellenistic Science and Culture in the Last Three Centuries B.C. Cambridge, Harvard University Press, 1959, p. 143.

2. Fremont Rider. The Scholar and the Future of the Research Library; A Problem and its Solution. New York, Hadham Press, 1944. Chapter 1.

3. For example Frederick C. Kent and Maude E. Kent, Compound Interest and Annuity Tables. New York, McGraw-Hill, 1926, pp. 14-44.

4. Keyes D. Metcalf. Planning Academic and Research Library Buildings. New York, McGraw-Hill, 1965, p. 155.

5. Fred J. Heinritz. "Predicting the Need for Catalog Expansion," Library Resources and Technical Services 11:247-8, 1967.

6. Herman H. Fussler and Julian L. Simon. Patterns in the Use of Books in Large Research Libraries. Chicago, University of Chicago Press, 1969, Chapter 5; and Fred J. Heinritz, Book Versus Card Catalog Costs (Ph.D. Dissertation) Rutgers University, 1963. Chapter XI.

7. For example, Kent and Kent, op. cit., pp. 46-73.

8. Fussler and Simon, op. cit.; and Ferdinand F. Leimkuhler, "Systems Analysis in University Libraries,"

College and Research Libraries 27:15, 1966.

9. Leimkuhler, op. cit., pp. 15-16.

Appendix

The derivation of equation (7) is based on the following three basic equations (8, 9, 10).

The first, the familar equation for amount at compound interest, is:

$$N_t = N_{t-1} (1 + i)$$
$$N_t = N_O (1 + i)^t \tag{8}$$

where N_t = the size of the collection at the end of year t

N_O = the size of the collection t years ago

i = the annual growth rate of the collection.

The second equation follows from the fact that $N_{t-1} = N_t/(1 + i)$:

$$A_t = N_t - N_{t-1}$$
$$A_t = N_{t-1} (1 + i) - N_{t-1}$$
$$A_t = N_{t-1} (i) \tag{9}$$
$$A_t = N_t (i/(1 + i))$$

where A_t = the acquisitions in year t.

The third equation is:

$$C_t (A_{t-j}) = C_O (1 - d)^j A_{t-j} \tag{10}$$

where $C_t (A_{t-j})$ = the circulation in year t of all books acquired in year (t - j)

C_O = the average circulation rate of all books acquired in year (t - j) in their first year of acquisition d = the annual circulation obsolescence rate.

The annual circulation of the entire collection, $C_t(N_t)$ is then defined as:

$$C_t(N_t) = C_t(A_t) + C_t(A_{t-1}) + \cdots + C_t(A_1) + C_t(N_O)$$

By use of equations (8), (9) and (10) $C_t(A_{t-j})$ can be defined in terms of N_O. The first t terms then form a geometric series, which is summed. Rearranging terms, we arrive at the equation:

$$C_t(N_t) = \frac{i\, C_O}{i+d}\, N_t + \frac{d\, C_O}{i+d}\, (1-d)^t\, N_O \qquad (11)$$

The equation for $C_t(N_{t-n})$ is derived in an analogous manner:

$$C_t(N_{t-n}) = \frac{i\, C_O}{i+d}\, N_t \left(\frac{1-d}{1+i}\right)^n = \frac{d\, C_O}{i+d}\, (1-d)^t\, N_O \qquad (12)$$

The second terms of equations (11) and (12) disappear, for practical purposes, for large t. Therefore:

Propcirc = Annual Circulation of Books Acquired More Than n Years Ago/Total Annual Circulation

$$\text{Propcirc} = \frac{i\, C_O}{i+d}\, N_t \left(\frac{1-d}{1+d}\right)^n \Big/ \frac{i\, C_O}{i+i}\, N_t$$

$$\text{Propcirc} = \left(\frac{1-d}{1+i}\right)^n$$

List of Figures

FIGURE 1

AMOUNT AT COMPOUND INTEREST $(1 + i)^n$

N	0.03	0.04	0.05	0.06	0.07	0.08	0.09	0.10	0.11	0.12
1	1.03	1.04	1.05	1.06	1.07	1.08	1.09	1.10	1.11	1.12
2	1.06	1.08	1.10	1.12	1.14	1.17	1.19	1.21	1.23	1.25
3	1.09	1.12	1.16	1.19	1.23	1.26	1.30	1.33	1.37	1.40
4	1.13	1.17	1.22	1.26	1.31	1.36	1.41	1.46	1.52	1.57
5	1.16	1.22	1.28	1.34	1.40	1.47	1.54	1.61	1.69	1.76
6	1.19	1.27	1.34	1.42	1.50	1.59	1.68	1.77	1.87	1.97
7	1.23	1.32	1.41	1.50	1.61	1.71	1.83	1.95	2.08	2.21
8	1.27	1.37	1.48	1.59	1.72	1.85	1.99	2.14	2.30	2.48
9	1.30	1.42	1.55	1.69	1.84	2.00	2.17	2.36	2.56	2.77
10	1.34	1.48	1.63	1.79	1.97	2.16	2.37	2.59	2.84	3.11
11	1.38	1.54	1.71	1.90	2.10	2.33	2.58	2.85	3.15	3.48
12	1.43	1.60	1.80	2.01	2.25	2.52	2.81	3.14	3.50	3.90
13	1.47	1.67	1.89	2.13	2.41	2.72	3.07	3.45	3.88	4.36
14	1.51	1.73	1.98	2.26	2.58	2.94	3.34	3.80	4.31	4.89
15	1.56	1.80	2.08	2.40	2.76	3.17	3.64	4.18	4.78	5.47

FIGURE 2

YEARS FROM THE PRESENT BEFORE CATALOG EXPANSION WILL BE NECESSARY

Q	ANNUAL RATE OF CATALOG GROWTH									
	1%	2%	3%	4%	5%	6%	7%	8%	9%	10%
1.05	4.9	2.5	1.7	1.2	1.0	0.8	0.7	0.6	0.6	0.5
1.10	9.6	4.8	3.2	2.4	2.0	1.6	1.4	1.2	1.1	1.0
1.15	14.0	7.1	4.7	3.6	2.9	2.4	2.1	1.8	1.6	1.5
1.20	18.3	9.2	6.2	4.6	3.7	3.1	2.7	2.4	2.1	1.9
1.25	22.4	11.3	7.5	5.7	4.6	3.8	3.3	2.9	2.6	2.3
1.30	26.4	13.2	8.9	6.7	5.4	4.5	3.9	3.4	3.0	2.8
1.35	30.2	15.2	10.2	7.7	6.2	5.2	4.4	3.9	3.5	3.1
1.40	33.8	17.0	11.4	8.6	6.9	5.8	5.0	4.4	3.9	3.5
1.45	37.3	18.8	12.6	9.5	7.6	6.4	5.5	4.8	4.3	3.9
1.50	40.8	20.5	13.7	10.3	8.3	7.0	6.0	5.3	4.7	4.3
1.55	44.0	22.1	14.8	11.2	9.0	7.5	6.5	5.7	5.1	4.6
1.60	47.2	23.7	15.9	12.0	9.6	8.1	6.9	6.1	5.5	4.9
1.65	50.3	25.3	16.9	12.8	10.3	8.6	7.4	6.5	5.8	5.3
1.70	53.3	26.8	18.0	13.5	10.9	9.1	7.8	6.9	6.2	5.6
1.75	56.2	28.3	18.9	14.3	11.5	9.6	8.3	7.3	6.5	5.9
1.80	59.1	29.7	19.9	15.0	12.0	10.1	8.7	7.6	6.8	6.2
1.85	61.8	31.1	20.8	15.7	12.6	10.6	9.1	8.0	7.1	6.5
1.90	64.5	32.4	21.7	16.4	13.2	11.0	9.5	8.3	7.4	6.7
1.95	67.1	33.7	22.6	17.0	13.7	11.5	9.9	8.7	7.7	7.0
2.00	69.7	35.0	23.4	17.7	14.2	11.9	10.2	9.0	8.0	7.3

Q = TOTAL CARD CAPACITY OF CATALOG/ PRESENT NUMBER OF CARDS IN CATALOG

FIGURE 3

PROPORTION OF A LIBRARY COLLECTION
IN SPECIAL STORAGE

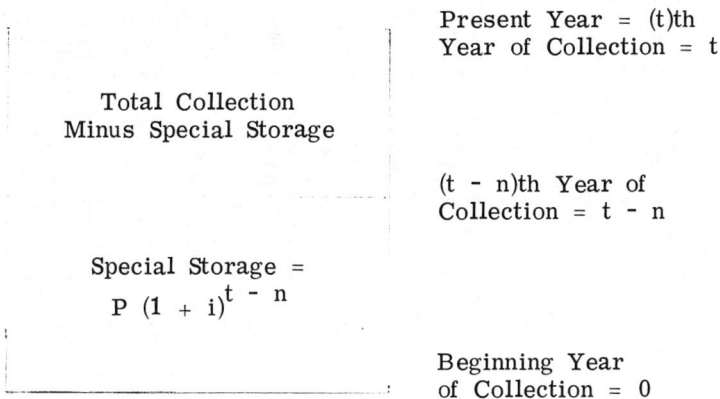

Present Year = (t)th
Year of Collection = t

Total Collection
Minus Special Storage

(t - n)th Year of
Collection = t - n

Special Storage =
$P (1 + i)^{t - n}$

Beginning Year
of Collection = 0

FIGURE 4

PRESENT VALUE $1/(1 + i)^n$

N	I									
	0.03	0.04	0.05	0.06	0.07	0.08	0.09	0.10	0.11	0.12
1	0.97	0.96	0.95	0.94	0.93	0.93	0.92	0.91	0.90	0.89
2	0.94	0.92	0.91	0.89	0.87	0.86	0.84	0.83	0.81	0.80
3	0.92	0.89	0.86	0.84	0.82	0.79	0.77	0.75	0.73	0.71
4	0.89	0.85	0.82	0.79	0.76	0.74	0.71	0.68	0.66	0.64
5	0.86	0.82	0.78	0.75	0.71	0.68	0.65	0.62	0.59	0.57
6	0.84	0.79	0.75	0.70	0.67	0.63	0.60	0.56	0.53	0.51
7	0.81	0.76	0.71	0.67	0.62	0.58	0.55	0.51	0.48	0.45
8	0.79	0.73	0.68	0.63	0.58	0.54	0.50	0.47	0.43	0.40
9	0.77	0.70	0.64	0.59	0.54	0.50	0.46	0.42	0.39	0.36
10	0.74	0.68	0.61	0.56	0.51	0.46	0.42	0.39	0.35	0.32
11	0.72	0.65	0.58	0.53	0.48	0.43	0.39	0.35	0.32	0.29
12	0.70	0.62	0.56	0.50	0.44	0.40	0.36	0.32	0.29	0.26
13	0.68	0.60	0.53	0.47	0.41	0.37	0.33	0.29	0.26	0.23
14	0.66	0.58	0.51	0.44	0.39	0.34	0.30	0.26	0.23	0.20
15	0.64	0.56	0.48	0.42	0.36	0.32	0.27	0.24	0.21	0.18

FIGURE 5

RELATIVE USE OF THE PROPORTION OF THE
COLLECTION IN SPECIAL STORAGE
FOR
D= 0. 05, I= 0. 06

AGE IN YEARS WHEN BOOK IS TRANSFERRED TO SPECIAL STORAGE	PROPORTION OF TOTAL COLLEC- TION IN SPECIAL STORAGE	PROPORTION OF THE TOTAL CIRCULATION FROM SPECIAL STORAGE
2	0.89	0.80
4	0.79	0.65
6	0.70	0.52
8	0.63	0.42
10	0.56	0.33
12	0.50	0.27
14	0.44	0.22
16	0.39	0.17
18	0.35	0.14
20	0.31	0.11
22	0.28	0.09
24	0.25	0.07
26	0.22	0.06
28	0.20	0.05
30	0.17	0.04
32	0.15	0.03
34	0.14	0.02
36	0.12	0.02
38	0.11	0.02
40	0.10	0.01

FIGURE 6

TABLE SOLVING $(1 - d)/(1 + i)$

I		D									
	0.030	0.040	0.050	0.060	0.070	0.080	0.090	0.100	0.110	0.120
0.030	0.942	0.932	0.922	0.913	0.903	0.893	0.883	0.874	0.864	0.854
0.040	0.933	0.923	0.913	0.904	0.894	0.885	0.875	0.865	0.856	0.846
0.050	0.924	0.914	0.905	0.895	0.886	0.876	0.867	0.857	0.848	0.838
0.060	0.915	0.906	0.896	0.887	0.877	0.868	0.858	0.849	0.840	0.830
0.070	0.907	0.897	0.888	0.879	0.869	0.860	0.850	0.841	0.832	0.822
0.080	0.898	0.889	0.880	0.870	0.861	0.852	0.843	0.833	0.824	0.815
0.090	0.890	0.881	0.872	0.862	0.853	0.844	0.835	0.826	0.817	0.807
0.100	0.882	0.873	0.864	0.855	0.845	0.836	0.827	0.818	0.809	0.800
0.110	0.874	0.865	0.856	0.847	0.838	0.829	0.820	0.811	0.802	0.793
0.120	0.866	0.857	0.848	0.839	0.830	0.821	0.813	0.804	0.795	0.786

FIGURE 7

PROPORTION OF CIRCULATION FROM SPECIAL STORAGE

$(1-D)/(1+I)$

N	0.765	0.800	0.815	0.830	0.845	0.860	0.875	0.890	0.905	0.920	0.935	0.950
2	0.616	0.640	0.664	0.689	0.714	0.740	0.766	0.792	0.819	0.846	0.874	0.902
4	0.380	0.410	0.441	0.475	0.510	0.547	0.586	0.627	0.671	0.716	0.764	0.815
6	0.234	0.262	0.293	0.327	0.364	0.405	0.449	0.497	0.549	0.606	0.668	0.735
8	0.144	0.168	0.195	0.225	0.260	0.299	0.344	0.394	0.450	0.513	0.584	0.663
10	0.089	0.107	0.129	0.155	0.186	0.221	0.263	0.312	0.369	0.434	0.511	0.599
12	0.055	0.069	0.086	0.107	0.133	0.164	0.201	0.247	0.302	0.368	0.446	0.540
14	0.034	0.044	0.057	0.074	0.095	0.121	0.154	0.196	0.247	0.311	0.390	0.488
16	0.021	0.028	0.038	0.051	0.068	0.090	0.118	0.155	0.202	0.263	0.341	0.440
18	0.013	0.018	0.025	0.035	0.048	0.066	0.090	0.123	0.166	0.223	0.298	0.397
20	0.008	0.012	0.017	0.024	0.034	0.049	0.069	0.097	0.136	0.189	0.261	0.358
22	0.005	0.007	0.011	0.017	0.025	0.036	0.053	0.077	0.111	0.160	0.228	0.324
24	0.003	0.005	0.007	0.011	0.018	0.027	0.041	0.061	0.091	0.135	0.199	0.292
26	0.002	0.003	0.005	0.008	0.013	0.020	0.031	0.048	0.075	0.114	0.174	0.264
28	0.001	0.002	0.003	0.005	0.009	0.015	0.024	0.038	0.061	0.097	0.152	0.238
30	0.001	0.001	0.002	0.004	0.006	0.011	0.018	0.030	0.050	0.082	0.133	0.215
32	0.000	0.001	0.001	0.003	0.005	0.008	0.014	0.024	0.041	0.069	0.116	0.194
34	0.000	0.001	0.001	0.002	0.003	0.006	0.011	0.019	0.034	0.059	0.102	0.175
36	0.000	0.000	0.001	0.001	0.002	0.004	0.008	0.015	0.028	0.050	0.089	0.158
38	0.000	0.000	0.000	0.001	0.002	0.003	0.006	0.012	0.023	0.042	0.078	0.142
40	0.000	0.000	0.000	0.001	0.001	0.002	0.005	0.009	0.018	0.036	0.068	0.129

TURNOVER RATE: BASIC LIBRARY
STATISTICS AND SOME APPLICATIONS

Theodore S. Huang

Libraries have been collecting statistics for many
years, and library statistics have been compiled and published since the 1870s. Each time a library is studied,
some statistics must be gathered and examined. Recent
years have witnessed more attempts at the definition and
evaluation of library statistics, and more critical comments
on the kind of statistics usually collected, compiled and
published. All agree that there are some library statistics
which every library should collect and which should be included in regular reporting on a national basis. Some more
detailed statistics, though not necessarily reported regularly
on a nationwide basis, should be compiled regularly for each
state and region. Needless to say, certain additional statistics must be gathered, often by sampling, in the evaluation
of an individual library.

Circulation statistics have been frequently collected.
In fact, it has been so common to see circulation figures
presented in library reports that sometimes they are regarded with a skeptical eye. One often hears circulation
figures mentioned in a derisive way when the staff size of a
public library branch and/or the allocation of book funds is
indeed based on circulation figures. Moreover, circulation
statistics are not considered to be comparable between libraries because of different loan periods, different restrictions on what may or may not be borrowed, differing methods of recording loans of titles in more than one volume,
and the variation in centralized or decentralized operations,
etc. [1] The joint conference of the International Federation of
Library Associations and the International Organization for
Standardization, held in Paris in October of 1967, made a
recommendation not to count loans for reasons relating to
either definition or possible misuse or misinterpretation of

circulation statistics.[2] Other library statistics also need
clear and precise definitions, and they are all subject to
misuse and misinterpretation. Such considerations should
not deter us from collecting basic library statistics in circulation or other areas. Circulation statistics should be
considered as basic library statistics, just as library collection statistics are. Basic library statistics of all kinds
should be collected and regularly reported, compiled and
published, because they are useful. They are indicative of
what we need and want to know about a library, even before
we have any fancier or more refined statistics, which probably only a survey or evaluation team will be able to obtain
or produce. The international conference of 1967 asserted
as the first reason for the omission of circulation statistics
that the "lending of books is important mainly (though not
entirely) in public lending libraries, and is relatively small
part of the work of most other types of library.[3] One can
take issue with this statement, and one can only wish that
the recommendation had been to include in regular reporting
circulation statistics for all types of libraries rather than
omit such statistics for even public libraries.

     The American Library Directory includes circulation
statistics for public libraries, but not for other types of libraries.[4] The National Center for Educational Statistics includes the total of loan transactions in the compilation of
statistics for public libraries,[5] but not in the compilation of
library statistics for colleges and universities.[6] This is
presumably in keeping with the 1966 handbook on Library
Statistics which recommended that "circulation statistics for
college and university libraries not be reported nationally."[7]
The Association of Research Libraries' compilation, Academic Library Statistics, does not include circulation figures,[8] although Downs' University Library Statistics, which
was assembled for the ARL-ACRL Joint Committee on University Library Statistics, does give such figures.[9]

     While the pattern is mixed, circulation statistics have
been frequently collected by libraries, and also studied. In
his book on the library's public, Berelson, using previous
studies, compared circulation and reference services, and
juvenile and adult book circulation, classified circulation by
form and subject matter, commented on circulation related
to currency and "quality," and attempted to relate users and
kinds of books circulated.[10] Carnovsky, considering circulation trends in public libraries, discussed various treat-
ments of circulation figures, such as circulation per capita,

by type of agency, by classes of material, and by reader.[11] Although, as Carnovsky noted, college and university library surveys have usually not been concerned with circulation statistics,[12] some attention has been given to circulation statistics in academic libraries. A few examples include the Nuffield pilot survey of library use in the University of Leeds,[13] the survey of borrowing from the Main Library at the University of Birmingham,[14] and Ritter's study of recorded library use in small four-year colleges during 1962-1963.[15] All of these, as did Downs' University Library Statistics, included the circulation per student statistic. The Nuffield pilot survey and the University of Birmingham Main Library survey were also concerned with faculty use and circulation by subject. Broadus studied faculty circulation,[16] and Radford student circulation by subject.[17] More recently, Donald Smith suggested three ways of sampling in estimating the annual circulation of the University of Oregon Library.[18]

Circulation statistics, like other library statistics, need clear and precise definition, and are subject to many variables. However, they are still indicative and should be among the basic library statistics to be collected and regularly reported, compiled and published. To illustrate how basic library statistics such as circulation and library collection statistics can be utilized, I shall discuss turnover rate.

Turnover rate (T) is the rate at which a library's collection is circulated in a year. $T = C/S$, where C is the library's total circulation, and S is the total items in the library collection. If we confine ourselves to books only, turnover rate (T) is the rate at which a library's book stock is circulated in a year. $T = C/S$, where C is the library's total circulation, and S is the total volumes of the book stock.[19]

A library's activities should be centered around the use of the library's collection. The evaluation of a library should be based on such use. Findings relative to such use not only help in the assessment of a library, but may assist in the allocation of funds and in collection development. For the academic library, circulation per capita, or per student or faculty member, is a statistic frequently observed, as mentioned before.[20] Yet, to focus on the use of a library's collection, we should utilize turnover rate which related directly a library's collection and its use.

The management of a library's collection has been referred to as inventory control. We should not want to have a large inventory on the simple assumption that the larger it is the better. A larger inventory is better only when it can meet the demand better. A larger inventory can be justified only when it is used at least as frequently as a smaller inventory, if not more frequently. The frequency of use should be viewed in relation to the size of the inventory. A simple measure of the frequency of use of a library's collection is its turnover rate.

For the purpose of illustration, let us take some figures from Downs' University Library Statistics. Table 1 gives the statistics for total circulation, total circulation per student, library's rank on total circulation per student, total volumes, turnover rate, and library's rank on turnover rate, for 34 academic libraries. [21] We are interested to know whether a higher total circulation per student results in a higher turnover rate. In other words, we wonder whether there is a correlation between the rank on total circulation per student and the rank on turnover rate. For the data in Table 1, the Spearman rank correlation coefficient is computed to be .27. The total circulation per student and the turnover rate have very low correlation. This is especially remarkable as the two statistics have the same total circulation figure as numerator. It is obvious that the rather low turnover rate for most of these academic libraries is the result of the sheer large size of their collections, which are not very actively used.

Figure 1 is a histogram for the ranks on turnover rate for the 34 academic libraries. The class with the largest number (9) of libraries in it is the class .305-.405. Next are the classes .105-.205 and .605-.705, with 6 libraries each. The University of Texas stands all alone, its turnover rate of 1.2366 being certainly unique. The median of these turnover rates is .3955.

Circulation and reserve as well as book collection statistics for six undergraduate libraries for 1964-1965 were given in Braden's The Undergraduate Library. [22] The turnover rate for each of these six undergraduate libraries, therefore, can be computed. Although the turnover rate computed for the entire university library as shown in Table 1 is for 1968, it is included in Table 2 just to give us some idea of the great difference in turnover rate between

(cont'd on p. 116)

Table 1

Total Circulation, Total Volumes, and
Turnover Rate for 34 Academic Libraries, 1968

University	A. Total Circulation	B. Total Circulation Per Student	C. Rank on B	D. Total Volumes	E. Turnover Rate	F. Rank on E
Brown	407,515	83.01	6	1,239,899	.3287	24
Cornell	1,249,895	86.38	3	3,257,399	.3837	19
Harvard	1,020,262	67.88	8	7,920,387	.1288	33
Indiana	1,350,000	49.82	13	1,846,551	.7311	4
Johns Hopkins	210,000	28.76	25	1,767,383	.1188	34
Louisiana State	196,466	10.24	34	1,045,454	.1879	30
M.I.T.	271,863	35.36	20	1,064,501	.2554	28
McGill	801,041	54.98	11	1,150,287	.6964	5
Michigan State	841,477	18.31	31	1,394,691	.6033	11
New York	811,002	36.38	18	1,534,610	.5285	14
Northwestern	262,509	16.38	32	1,936,782	.1355	32
Ohio State	1,388,691	34.18	21	2,103,723	.6601	8
Pennsylvania State	760,779	21.34	30	1,164,142	.6535	9
Princeton	515,234	109.18	1	1,998,491	.2578	27
Purdue	625,280	22.49	27	903,748	.6919	6
Stanford	1,034,314	91.39	2	3,070,812	.3368	22
Tulane	525,154	59.60	9	984,258	.5336	12

Univ. Arizona	628,549	31.03	23	1,291,778	.4866	15
California, Berkeley	2,361,329	84.88	5	3,478,893	.6788	7
California, LA	1,989,660	68.44	7	2,610,572	.7622	2
Colorado	777,801	45.47	14	1,202,337	.6469	10
Florida	959,842	58.55	10	1,273,515	.7537	3
Illinois	1,562,740	54.54	12	4,086,854	.3824	20
Iowa	407,185	24.09	26	1,389,108	.2931	26
Kansas	532,343	33.62	22	1,344,739	.3959	17
Kentucky	194,453	14.35	33	969,360	.2006	29
Michigan	1,263,434	35.95	19	3,816,394	.3311	23
Minnesota	1,063,017	22.02	28	2,691,202	.3950	18
North Carolina	583,241	37.41	17	1,821,756	.3202	25
Oklahoma	610,626	38.21	16	1,153,758	.5293	13
Southern California	491,706	41.53	15	1,290,862	.3809	21
Texas	2,517,704	85.27	4	2,036,000	1.2366	1
Univ. Virginia	261,096	30.47	24	1,445,229	.1807	31
Wayne State	536,962	21.56	29	1,110,592	.4835	16

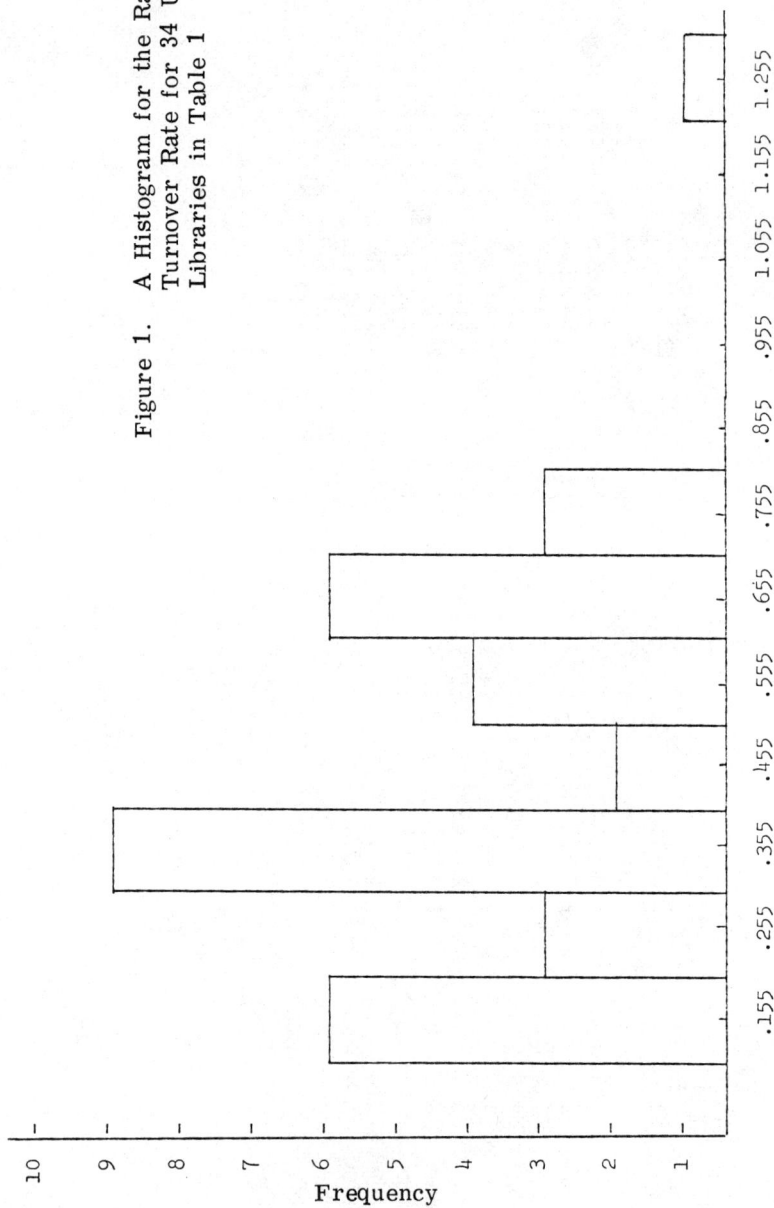

Figure 1. A Histogram for the Ranks on Turnover Rate for 34 University Libraries in Table 1

Table 2

Total Circulation, Total Volumes, Turnover Rate
of Undergraduate Library, and Turnover Rate of
Entire University Library in Six Universities

University	Total Circulation of Undergraduate Library[23]	Total Volumes of Undergraduate Library	Turnover Rate of Undergraduate Library	Turnover Rate of Entire University Library[25]
Harvard	317,661	142,091	2.24	.1288
Univ. Michigan	1,028,084	120,080	8.56	.3311
Univ. South Carolina	67,451	36,336	1.86	---
Indiana	240,370	39,916	6.02	.7311
Cornell	239,873	57,103	4.20	.3837
Univ. Texas	732,25924	71,419	10.25	1.2366

undergraduate libraries and university libraries as a whole.
The median of the six undergraduate libraries' turnover
rates is 5.11.

Turnover rate can serve as a guide in collection development as to the assignment of priorities to various subjects, together with examination of existing collections, analysis of interlibrary loans, follow-up of curriculum development, and accreditation requirements, etc. From the use
point of view, the higher the turnover rate of a subject collection is, the more worthwhile it is to build it up. If each
of the subjects has a sizable collection of standard and current books, the turnover rate of each subject collection can
be very revealing, especially in the light of the courses offered in the subject area, and the number of students and of
teachers associated with the courses. While circulation alone
shows the frequency of use, turnover rate indicates the frequency of use as related to the size of the collection. In
allocating book funds, turnover rate can be used as an adjusting factor taking into account both present use and past
acquisitions. The use of turnover rate in the allocation of
book funds may help avoid continuing simply to spend in the
same way as in the past, as has often been the practice.
Big spending in subject areas where there has been no real
need and/or where book selection has been poor will be
penalized, as the low turnover rate will result in less book
funds allocated to those subject areas. We will get away
from huge collections, away from getting bigger just for the
sake of getting bigger, knowing that bigger is not necessarily
better. When turnover rate is low, it is a warning signal.
There are many possible reasons, and, therefore, many
things need to be looked into. Instead of sitting pretty with
a large collection, we must conduct some investigations, do
some hard thinking, and make some hard decisions as well.

For the purpose of illustration, Table 3 presents data
on total circulation, total number of volumes, turnover rate,
percentage by total circulation, and percentage by turnover
rate, by LC class, for one academic library for the calendar
year 1973. Table 4 gives the results of four different ways
of allocating book funds. The first is by a certain formula,
named Y formula in the table, based on the level of collecting, the content of the curriculum, and the way the teaching
departments are structured. Table 4 also gives the results
of allocating book funds by total circulation and by adjusting
the Y formula computation by total circulation. These are
included for the purpose of comparison. The D Column in
(cont'd on p. 123)

Table 3

Total Circulation, Total Volumes, Turnover Rate,
and Percentage for X Academic Library, 1973

LC Classes		A. Total Circulation Jan.-Dec. 1973	B. Total Volumes 12/31/73	C. Turnover Rate	D. % by Total Circ.	E. % by Turnover Rate
B, BC, BD BH-BX	Philosophy, Religion	536	1,776	.3018	.0584	.0231
BF	Psychology	687	845	.8130	.0748	.0622
C, D, E, F	History	857	4,094	.2093	.0934	.0160
G, GA-GF	Geography	47	144	.3264	.0051	.0250
GN-GT	Anthropology	36	161	.2236	.0039	.0171
GV	Recreation	50	143	.3497	.0055	.0268
H	Social Sciences	30	111	.2703	.0033	.0207
HA	Statistics	29	93	.3118	.0032	.0239
HB-HJ	Economics	652	2,334	.2794	.0710	.0214
HM-HX	Sociology	842	1,374	.6128	.0917	.0469
J	Political Science	196	1,232	.1591	.0214	.0122

Table 3 (Cont'd)

LC Classes		A. Total Circulation Jan.-Dec. 1973	B. Total Volumes 12/31/73	C. Turnover Rate	D. % by Total Circ.	E. % by Turnover Rate
K	Law	71	574	.1237	.0077	.0095
L	Education	764	3,687	.2072	.0832	.0159
M	Music	94	429	.2191	.0102	.0168
N	Fine Arts	287	846	.3392	.0313	.0260
P, PA-PM	Languages, Classical and Non-European Literatures	244	1,051	.2322	.0266	.0178
PN	Literary History and Collections (General)	217	1,230	.1764	.0236	.0135
PQ	Romance Literatures	143	569	.2513	.0156	.0192
PR	English Literature	357	2,110	.1692	.0389	.0129
PS	American Literature	391	979	.3994	.0426	.0306
PT	Germanic Literatures	72	281	.2563	.0078	.0196
PZ	Fiction	85	111	.7658	.0093	.0586

Q	Science (General)	92	233	.3949	.0100	.0302
QA	Mathematics	319	916	.3483	.0348	.0266
QB, QC	Astronomy, Physics	238	683	.3485	.0259	.0267
QD	Chemistry	122	635	.1921	.0133	.0147
QE	Geology	23	49	.4694	.0025	.0359
QH-QR	Natural History, Biology	710	1,487	.4775	.0773	.0365
R	Medicine	524	787	.6658	.0571	.0509
S	Agriculture	23	156	.1474	.0025	.0113
T	Technology (General) Industrial Engineering	71	93	.7634	.0077	.0584
TA-TH	General Engineering, Civil Engineering	137	335	.4090	.0149	.0313
TJ, TL	Mechanical Engineering	26	121	.2149	.0028	.0164
TK	Electrical Engineering	78	336	.2321	.0085	.0178
TN-TR	Chemical Engineering	74	219	.3379	.0081	.0259
TS, TT	Manufactures, Handicrafts	20	48	.4167	.0022	.0319
TX	Home Economics	14	31	.4516	.0015	.0346
U, V	Military Science, Naval Science	23	111	.2072	.0025	.0159

Table 4

Allocation of Book Funds by LC Classes

LC Classes		A. By Y Formula	B. by Total Circulation	C. A Adjusted by Total Circulation	D. A Adjusted by Turnover Rate
B, BC, BD BH-BX	Philosophy, Religion	$ 1,391.32	$ 2,803.20	$ 1,907.35	$ 1,190.37
BF	Psychology	2,434.81	3,590.40	4,275.21	5,609.07
C, D, E, F	History	2,434.81	4,483.20	5,338.29	1,442.85
G, GA-GF	Geography	695.66	244.80	83.29	644.15
GN-GT	Anthropology	695.66	187.20	63.69	440.59
GV	Recreation	347.83	264.00	44.91	345.26
H	Social Sciences	695.66	158.40	53.90	533.37
HA	Statistics	695.66	153.60	52.25	615.78
HB-HJ	Economics	3,826.13	3,408.00	6,376.88	3,032.56
HM-HX	Sociology	2,434.81	4,401.60	5,241.13	4,229.37
J	Political Science	1,391.32	1,027.20	698.92	628.66

K	Law	244.78	125.99	369.60	695.66
L	Education	2,253.19	7,472.63	3,993.60	3,826.13
M	Music	422.82	166.57	489.60	695.66
N	Fine Arts	1,339.78	1,022.25	1,502.40	1,391.32
P, PA-PM	Languages, Classical and Non-European Literatures	917.26	868.76	1,276.80	1,391.32
PN	Literary History and Collections (General)	347.82	385.40	1,132.80	695.66
PQ	Romance Literatures	494.70	254.74	748.80	695.66
PR	English Literature	664.74	1,270.47	1,867.20	1,391.32
PS	American Literature	2,759.44	2,434.81	2,044.80	2,434.81
PT	Germanic Literatures	478.85	127.37	374.40	695.66
PZ	Fiction	1,509.85	151.88	446.40	695.66
Q	Science (General)	389.07	81.64	480.00	347.83
QA	Mathematics	2,398.74	1,988.99	1,670.40	2,434.81
QB, QC	Astronomy, Physics	1,375.85	845.89	1,243.20	1,391.32
QD	Chemistry	757.48	434.39	638.40	1,391.32
QE	Geology	462.48	20.42	120.00	347.83
QH-QR	Natural History, Biology	3,291.52	4,418.10	3,710.40	2,434.81
R	Medicine	1,311.44	932.44	2,740.80	695.66

Table 4 (Cont'd)

LC Classes		A. By Y Formula	B. by Total Circulation	C. A Adjusted by Total Circulation	D. A Adjusted by Turnover Rate
S	Agriculture	$ 347.83	$ 120.00	$ 20.42	$ 145.59
T	Technology (General), Industrial Engineering	1,391.32	369.60	251.48	3,009.37
TA-TH	General Engineering, Civil Engineering	695.66	715.20	24.34	806.44
TJ, TL	Mechanical Engineering	1,391.32	134.40	91.46	845.11
TK	Electrical Engineering	1,391.32	408.00	277.61	917.26
TN-TR	Chemical Engineering	695.66	388.80	132.28	667.33
TS, TT	Manufactures, Handicrafts	695.66	105.60	35.94	821.93
TX	Home Economics	347.83	72.00	12.25	445.74
U, V	Military Science Naval Science	347.83	120.00	20.42	204.85
	Total	$48,000.54	$48,004.80	$48,004.76	$47,995.49

Table 4 lists the book funds allocated to LC classes by using
turnover rate as an adjusting factor. All figures are given
in dollars and cents to show the computation in more detail.
In the actual allocation of book funds, the figures can be
rounded to the nearest dollar.

The differences can be readily seen. Column D figures are most reasonable, for they not only take into account both the use and size of the collection, but also avoid
many small amounts allocated, as in the case of Column B
and Column C figures.

Turnover rate is a measure of the frequency of use
of a library's collection. It is a good indicator in our assessment of a library. By applying turnover rate, we can
evaluate as a first step the adequacy of a library collection.
It can flash a warning signal. The application of turnover
rate provides one guide, among others, in assigning priorities
to various subjects for collection development. Turnover
rate can be applied as an adjusting factor in the allocation
of book funds. In addition, as turnover rate varies among
libraries, it can possibly serve as a measure by which libraries can be grouped. Are there variations in turnover
rate by types of libraries? By sizes? By regions? Or,
is there a norm in turnover rate among all libraries? Thus,
turnover rate, a simple measure derived from two basic library statistics, total circulation and total collection size,
can be very useful, in typology, in evaluation, and in resource allocation.

Notes

1. Neil A. Radford. "The Problems of Academic Library
    Statistics," Library Quarterly 38:245, 1968. Library
    Statistics: A Handbook of Concepts, Definitions, and
    Terminology. Chicago, American Library Associa-
    tion, 1966, p. 22.

2. K. A. Mallaber, Torben Nielsen, and F. W. Torrington,
    eds. The International Standardization of Library
    Statistics: A Progress Report. London, International
    Federation of Library Associations, 1968, pp. 73, 74.

3. Ibid., p. 73.

4. American Library Directory, 1972-1973. N.Y., Bowker,
    1972.

5. Statistics of Public Libraries Serving Areas With at
    Least 25,000 Inhabitants, 1968. Washington, D.C.,
    National Center for Educational Statistics, 1970.

6. Library Statistics of Colleges and Universities, Institu-
    tional Data, Fall 1971, Part A & Part B. Washing-
    ton, D.C., National Center for Educational Statis-
    tics, 1972.

7. Library Statistics, op. cit., p. 22.

8. Academic Library Statistics, 1972-1973. Washington,
    D.C., Association of Research Libraries, 1973.

9. Robert B. Downs. University Library Statistics.
    Chicago, American Library Association, 1970.

10. Bernard Berelson. The Library's Public. N.Y.,
    Columbia Univ. Press, 1949, pp. 51-69.

11. Leon Carnovsky. "Survey of the Use of Library Re-
    sources and Facilities," in Maurice F. Tauber and
    Irene Roemer Stephens, eds., Library Surveys.
    N.Y., Columbia Univ. Press, 1967, pp. 72 ff.

12. Carnovsky, op. cit., p. 86.

13. B. S. Page and P. E. Tucker. "The Nuffield Pilot
    Survey of Library Use in the University of Leeds,"
    Journal of Documentation 15:1-11, 1959.

14. K. W. Humphreys. "Survey of Borrowing from the
    Main Library, the University of Birmingham,"
    Libri 14:126-35, 1964.

15. R. Vernon Ritter. "Recorded Library Use in Small
    Four-Year Colleges, 1962-1963," College & Re-
    search Libraries 25:391-2, 1964.

16. Robert N. Broadus. "An Analysis of Faculty Circula-
    tion in a University Library," College & Research
    Libraries 24:323-5, 1963.

17. Neil A. Radford. "Student Borrowing from a University
    Library," Australian Library Journal 15:154-60, 1966.

18. Donald T. Smith. "Circulation Statistics by Sampling,"

in Irene Braden Hoadley and Alise S. Clark, eds.,
Quantitative Methods in Librarianship. Westport,
Conn., Greenwood Press, 1972, pp. 214-16.

19. For purposes of illustration, let us confine ourselves
to books only. The same approach can be applied
to other types of library materials. Also, for purposes of illustration, we do not deal with in-library
use here, except for the use of reserve books.
Circulation means here outside-library use and the
use of reserve books. It has been found that there
is a high correlation between in-library use and outside-library use of books by subject. McGrath
found the correlation to be .86 or .84 (Pearson
product-moment correlation coefficient), and I have
found the correlation to be .92 (Spearman rank correlation coefficient). See William E. McGrath,
"Correlating the Subjects of Books Taken Out of and
Books Used Within an Open-Stack Library," College
& Research Libraries 32:280-5, 1971.

20. The "effective circulations per user," as expounded in
the recent Performance Measures for Public Libraries, is similar, only with both in-library use
and outside-library circulation taken into account.
See Ernest R. De Prospo, et al. Performance
Measures for Public Libraries. Chicago, American
Library Association, 1973, pp. 38-49.

21. Downs, op. cit. The "Total Circulation" figures are
the same as "General and Reserve Circulation," and
the "Total Circulation Per Student" figures are the
same as "General and Reserve Circulation (Per
Capita)" in Table XXXVII, pp. 84-86. The "Total
Volumes" are taken from Table XXX, pp. 63-65.
Sixteen other libraries included in these tables are
omitted here as their figures were either not available or apparently not comparable for reasons given
in the notes to these tables. The libraries' ranks
on total circulation per student and on turnover rate
as well as their turnover rate were computed by me.

22. Irene A. Braden. The Undergraduate Library. Chicago, American Library Association, 1970. Statistics for a number of years were given in this book,
the latest being for 1964-1965.

23. All figures for the undergraduate libraries are from
    Braden's book, and these figures in Table 2 are for
    1964-65. The total circulation includes circulation
    and reserve statistics.

24. The total circulation figure of 732,259 for 1964-1965 is
    from Table 38 in Braden's book, p. 134. The cir-
    culation and reserve figures in Tables 35 and 36
    (p. 132) add to only 722,934 for 1964-1965.

25. The turnover rate for the entire university library is
    based on 1968 figures given in Downs' Unversity
    Library Statistics, which does not include figures
    for the University of South Carolina.

QUALI-QUANTI AS OUTPUT PERFORMANCE CRITERIA

Choong H. Kim

Librarians are under pressure to gather statistical data on library operations and uses.[1] They do indeed gather masses of data, often for the sake of record keeping and for fact finding. As for what to do with those masses of factual data, there have been many studies which have attempted to develop library performance measures. The latest of these is the Public Library Association's Performance Measure for Public Libraries by E. R. De Prospo and others.[2] In addition to their conclusions about the weaknesses of many previous measurement studies, the authors point out that the most glaring weakness is that most of the attempts were "thing-oriented" rather than "user-oriented." Even the latest output-oriented studies, such as Morris Hamburg's "document exposure" measures,[3] are not really "user-oriented" because performance is equated to such questions as: "How much has the library produced?" rather than "How well has the user been using the service?"

The purpose of this essay is to explore the idea that the quality of library service may be definable and, therefore, measurable in the following four service areas in terms of User Performance, for which the evaluative criteria is the degree of user's success in completing the defined task using the defined program offered; and in terms of User Productivity, for which the evaluative criteria are the amount of time and effort (including expenses) that have been required of the user for using the program for the defined task:

Materials Domain:

   1) Adequacy of material resources of the library--
      a measure in user success;

127

2) Delivery of materials and material reproducing
services--a measure in user productivity.

Intellectual Domain:

3) Intellectual (or bibliographical) organization produced by the library--a measure in user
success;

4) Professional staff assistance--a measure in user
productivity.

The proposed evaluation criteria of performance are
not designed to produce a single measure, nor are they designed to measure the effect of library use on the user's research results or learning achievement, such as grade point
averages, because, considering the very complex nature of
human intellectual processes and varying individual needs,
it is highly unlikely that any single, overall measure of performance and/or productivity can be found to evaluate the
library or libraries, programs, and individual users altogether. If there were one single measure, it would be a
naive and perhaps dangerous oversimplification of a very
complex, value-laden human endeavor of "evaluation." It is
unrealistic to expect that one can measure the effect of library use on the user's learning or research results, for the
library professionals are not normally given the primary responsibility or control over the research or learning processes and results. At best, the librarian has a shared role
in such processes and, therefore, a shared credit. The proposed criteria have been made deliberately simple and un-
arithmatical, for evaluation rather than measurement is emphasized. One could use the proposed criteria alone or in
combination with any other input or capability measures.

Basic Parameters for Users,
Libraries, and Institutions

Paul Samuelson's definition of economic science is applicable in discussing the basic constraining parameters
wherein all must operate. This is admittedly a macrosystem view of library services. For example, users' individual disposable time, the amount of material they have to
handle, and their intellectual interest, ability, and capacity
are viewed as scarce resources; by the same token, libraries' material resources, staff expertise, physical

facilities, equipment and machines, and parent institutions' total brain and material reserves, technical facilities and human organization are all viewed as scarce resources to be managed rationally. However, the library departs from economics in that it is not a business enterprise whose main concerns are profit and continuing growth.

The user cannot stretch the disposable time except by making it more productive and rewarding. The user cannot and need not use all the pertinent material. He must select the best or the most appropriate. The community of users is viewable as a macrosystem wherein one's use of a library service affects others' use of the service. For example, if one checks out a book for so long, everyone else who needs the book will be forced to spend time and effort trying to find it. Time is increasingly costly and it seems to be the most important factor as far as users are concerned. When asked to rank the services they preferred to receive, given a certain amount of gift money or budget increase, users of the M.I.T. Libraries ranked a cheaper rate Xerox service first, and LC messenger and added reserve copies as second and third, respectively. [4]

The library has been viewed as a single, general purpose system. In fact it is a macrosystem consisting of multiple programs wherein each program competes with others for funds, staff and, above all, user patronage. The latter is important, inasmuch as the user, after all, is the best judge of his or her own performance in using the services offered. The potential user demand for service, especially public service could easily exceed the available staff or resources. In such a case, the latter must be rationed, as most libraries in fact have been doing. Traditional library standards have specified what the minimum rations of various resources and services should be. Given limited resources and a limited operating budget, the library must try to make them go as far as they can.

For many years it has been clear to the librarian that the single-library paradigm has to be dropped or modified in favor of a multiple-library system paradigm, for the library does not and cannot function in isolation. People now have multiple access to multiple sources of information. Given today's enormous library resources and the communication and transportation facilities available for use by people, it is increasingly necessary to deal with multiple libraries rather than with a single library. The community of multiple libraries is a macrosystem wherein one library's performance does directly and indirectly affect other libraries' performance. The interlibrary relationship in such a system is often competitive rather than coordinative. A case in point is the traditional relationship between the school and the public libraries in the same community. The same kind of closed-system relationship applies to the multi-state system or to the whole nation, and increasingly to the whole world.

User Performance

        User performance means how successfully and how productively the user has made use of library service for a given purpose or task within the constraints of available time and ability. It is not how many books one has used but how productive one has been. With this definition, the basic premise from which the proposed criteria are derived is that the library performance is a composite function of user-performance. The former is relative to the latter, for library performance cannot be determined without regard to varying user needs and ability. The performance is an actual quality, not a hypothetical one such as "capability," which is often mistaken for an output quality.

        Many would suggest that user satisfaction be used as the output measure. This poses a difficult problem in that, as everyone knows, satisfaction is an inverse function of expectation, and the most satisfied patrons may be the least demanding ones.

        Orr, Ping and others have done a good bit of work in developing performance measures in the area of biomedical library services. One notable effort has been the development of the concept of "document delivery capability," and the effort to test such measures.[5] Orr has also suggested that the criteria to determine the "measure of goodness" should be expressable in "quality" or "capability of resources," and "value" or "beneficial effects of utilization."[6] He has further suggested that an overall "global" measure may possibly be developed to account for all output. The latter presents formidable problems, and "capability" is in fact an input quality. In other words, it merely indicates a potential like an electric "voltage" value, not a work done measure like the electrical "wattage."

Adequacy of Material Resources--
A Measure in User Success

This criterion deals with the adequacy of material resources in the defined library for the defined community of
users. One question is foremost in the user's mind: "Would
I find the material I know I want in the library?" This may
be a single library or a group of libraries. In the latter
case, the question would be: "Would I find the material I
want anywhere in the state or in the country?"

Development of a local library collection in a given
program or subject area appropriate for the defined local
community is among the oldest and most usual expectations
people have of a library. Performance on resources development from the user's standpoint is not in terms of how
large the collection is, but how relevant to the user. A
good learning resources collection is highly relevant to a
school community, a good local history collection to a local
town, and a Harvard-Yenching collection to the nation's and
the world's scholarly community.

The adequacy and relevancy of the material resources
may be measurable in terms of the degree of success the
users have experienced in finding the desired material in the
collection. This may be called "user success rate," an
actual quality, not a hypothetical quality of the so-called
"document delivery capability," which is often derived by
simulation involving hypothetical users making hypothetical
requests.

Some have used the term "success rate" to indicate
the collection's potential capability based on the size of the
collection in percentages of the total body of material available either in the market or in a standard catalog. This
cannot indicate directly what people actually wanted and what
they got in the collection. Size, along with "up-to-dateness"
of the collection, however, functions as an independent contributing variable that should indeed influence user success.
The total circulation count as an output measure is meaningful only in a business sense--the more, the better.

Some usable data may be found in many unrelated
studies. Urquart and Schofield of Cambridge University Library used this measure, which they termed "shelf failure
rate," with much practicability.[7] It is used in the report
of the books by mail programs that are operating in a number of public libraries.[8]

Delivery of Materials and Services--
A Measure in User Productivity

        It is one thing for the user to have access in the li-
brary to the world's best collection on, say, Dreiser, but it
is another for him to get to the collection and put his hands
on it. Two questions are prominent in the user's mind:
a) How long (days, weeks, etc.) must one wait to obtain the
desired material (one knows exactly what one wants) from
local or other libraries through any of the delivery means?
b) How much expenditure of time, labor and money is required of one to call or to get to the library and to the
shelves?

        User productivity is measurable in terms of time and
effort (including money expenses) actually required of the
user to obtain the wanted material by such means as home
delivery, mail, telephone or teletype, or by walking into the
library. The time spent in the library is viewed as a necessary expense--the shorter, the better, provided that the
given task is completed. Two independent variables, library
delivery capability and user capability, can directly influence
user productivity. User capability (or familiarity), is, perhaps, more significant than library capability.

        The use of the library's physical facilities is viewed
as an independent variable having a direct relationship, up to
a certain point, with all aspects of user performance. The
library quarters must be adequate and functional, but abundant space and luxurious furnishing do not necessarily help
user productivity, and, in fact, may have a contrary effect.
Spatial, functional, and aesthetic efficiency are essential, but
they are not an output in themselves, unless the library is
viewed as a space-renting business.

        Usable data may be found in some scattered sources. [9-12]
While outside loan data are abundant, inside-use data are difficult to find in the literature. Data on the number of users
in the library at a given time and on how long they stay have
been gathered mainly for the purpose of studying the use of
library space. [13-15] Such data usually indicate peak hours of
the day, crowding conditions of various floor areas, and the
average length of time the users stay in the library.

Intellectual (Bibliographical) Organization Produced
by the Library--A Measure in User Success

    The library is a place where people come to get their
knowledge renewed, their thoughts reorganized, and their
spirit replenished by reading and examining other people's
thoughts and experiences. What is the librarian's direct professional contribution to these intellectual processes? It is
in the form of the library-produced bibliographic organization that contributes directly to helping users make the most
of these intellectual processes. This bibliographic service
belongs in the professional, intellectual domain, in contrast
to the previously discussed services which belong in the materials domain.

    Four bibliographic problems are foremost in the user's
mind: a) How to locate the desired material in the local as
well as other libraries; b) How to select from among numerous choices the most desirable or appropriate material;
c) How to get informed of new developments in one's field,
or, on the current state of the art in one's field; d) How
to discover or get help in discovering or formulating new
ideas, models, hypotheses, and/or new questions. User
performance with regard to the use of library-produced bibliographical tools (library catalogs, subject bibliographies,
indexes, abstracts, current awareness, selective dissemination of information services, etc.) is relative to user ability,
need, and purpose or task at a given time, and is measurable by the user's own judgment of how successful he/she
was in using a specific bibliographical tool for a given task
at a given time. This may be done over a period of time.
A simple scale rating method may be used to reveal all-
user success rate with regard to each different tool or different purpose or task.

    The information science literature seems to indicate
that there is a common matrix of evaluation measures (or
criteria) of performance of information systems. The pro-
liferation of measures seems to be the result of different
combinations of criteria proposed by different individuals
from widely different points of view or emphases. John A.
Swets[16] discussed ten different measures, as did M. Cooper[17]
in his thesis. The common matrix is a two-by-two contin-
gency table of pertinence (or relevancy) versus retrieval of
documents and/or that of cost and value in terms of time

and convenience. The cost is to the library and the value to
the user, but when the effectiveness measure and the cost-
benefit measure are combined, one gets a confusing picture.

The proposed measure in terms of user success as
assessed by the user's own judgment is, for all practical
purposes, sufficient to indicate the effectiveness of the bibliographical tools as far as the user is concerned. This
can bypass all the difficulties of an "objective" performance
measure that tries to determine or fix all kinds of "system
capabilities" as well as "benefits" to the two competing interest groups, the library and the user, in a single all-pur-
pose measure. A few data samples on effectiveness of bibliographical tools and services may be cited.[18-22]

Professional Staff Assistance--
A Measure in User Productivity

The user's problems that require direct professional
staff assistance are the same as those bibliographical prob-
lems--locating, selecting, state of the art and/or keeping
up-to-date, and discovering. The professional staff is responsible for providing intellectual assistance (not directional
assistance), first through the ready-made library-produced
intellectual (or more descriptively, bibliographical) organization, and second, through direct help, either explaining the
use of bibliographical tools or dispensing or imparting the
information and knowledge directly. Whichever the case, the
professional takes the credit as well as the blame by assuming requisite authority and responsibility for the information
service. If bibliographical assistance is concerned with user
success, direct assistance is concerned with user productivity,
making sure that the user has made the most of the intellectual service provided with a minimum of unproductive effort.
In fact many libraries have asked users to comment on how
helpful the staff was.[23,24]

In intellectual service, user productivity is directly
related to the competency level of the staff. This is the intellectual domain where professional competency or capability
can be translated directly into quality of output. The efficacy
of staff subject specialization is not unlike that in medical
practice--people can expect better quality treatment from a
group practice than from a single general practitioner.

User productivity may be measured by asking users

to rate how intellectually helpful the staff has been to them
in accomplishing a defined task.   It is the librarian's responsibility to differentiate finely and meaningfully the intellectual
assistance that the staff is capable of giving to the user.
Above all, the staff must advertise such capabilities so that
users can expect more from the staff and can accomplish
more.

The literature on the measurement and evaluation of
reference service indicates not only the lack of commonly
accepted purpose and evaluative criteria, but confusion over
professional responsibility and authority.   This state of confusion gives rise to the general quandary in which reference
librarians find themselves.   Terry Weech observed that
"much of the literature still concentrates on measurement
rather than evaluation."[25] If the reference staff is not clear
about program goals, nor about the authority and responsibility they have, the users can hardly be expected to know
what they can reasonably expect from the staff.

In fact, the term "reference" is an anachronism, for
a mature profession, such as law or medicine, does not ter-
minate the service after referring the client to an authorita-
tive "source."   They are themselves the "source."   Some
perceive this as a semantic or communication problem between the staff and the user rather than a confusion over
staff roles.[26,27]

A number of studies have attempted to evaluate reference service in terms of accuracy and/or breadth of information that is obtainable from the reference staff.[28-30] Although these studies indicate a welcome new direction in
evaluation, one still gets confused about the hypothetical
quality of "reference capability" being translated directly into
actual output quality.   The latter can only be measured by
actual use by actual users, not by simulation using hypothetical test questions.

Summary Observation

The four measures discussed so far will be summarized by each user in a general feeling about the quality of
library service and about how well his/her need can be met
in and by the library.   This may be the eventual output that
really counts.   This is very much like how people evaluate
health care services.   The question, "Is anyone not getting

the service for any extrinsic reasons?" should be asked for
each defined library program.

      The Quali-Quanti is a quantitative expression of qual-
ity. Facts or numbers do not and cannot speak for themselves. They have to be interpreted and understood by their
users. However, this does not diminish the necessity or
value of gathering factual data upon which an evaluation may
be based. The quality is defined and expressed not in numbers but in scales, in ratios, in percentages, in percentiles,
or in coefficients. Magnitudes, such as time, monies, costs,
material resources, are meaningful only in relation to their
use by the user. The magnitude of use is meaningful only
in relation to the quality of use about which only the user
can make the best judgment.

      Consistency and uniformity of meaning are essential
in the application of any measure among its users whether
one uses it for one system or for multiple systems. One
should be extremely wary of implications in comparing systems. A branch library should not be closed because it does
not perform as well as others. A program such as bookmobile service should not be dropped because books by mail
is performing better. Each system, branch, or program
has a unique purpose and unique advantages, against which
the system or the program should be evaluated.

      In management by objectives, staff members are
evaluated not against one another but against the objective
set up by the parties directly involved. The same principle
should apply in evaluation of systems, programs, or libraries. Where multiple-library comparison is done, it is
done for the purpose of finding out how one stands in relation to others and/or how each of several variables under
study is distributed among the many that are studied. For
want of any absolute criteria or precisely defined objectives,
such comparison methods, often involving higher sophisticated
statistical analyses, are used as a rationale for determining
the size and growth rate of a system, program, collection,
staff, etc. Stanley McElderry discussed various comparison
methods that have been used by university libraries.[31] As
he pointed out in his concluding discussion, the size and
growth rate or the overall parameters within which the program or system must operate are often determined in a political context, but there is still a large area where how one
prepares the figures in presenting one's budget makes a
difference.

Notes

1. Summary of major recommendations in American Li-
    brary Association. Library Administration Division.
    Planning for a Nationwide System of Library Statis-
    tics. Washington, Government Printing Office, 1970,
    p. 1.

2. Ernest R. De Prospo, Ellen Altman, and Kenneth
    Beasley. Performance Measures for Public Li-
    braries. Chicago, American Library Association,
    1973.

3. Morris Hamburg, et al. A Systems Analysis of the
    Library and Information Science Statistical Data
    System: The Research Investigation. Philadelphia,
    University of Pennsylvania, 1970. Part I.

4. J. A. Raffel and R. Shishko. Systematic Analysis of
    University Libraries: An Application of Cost-Bene-
    fit Analysis to the M. I. T. Libraries. Cambridge,
    The M. I. T. Press, 1969, p. 99.

5. Richard H. Orr, et al. "Development of Methodologic
    Tools for Planning and Managing Library Serivces,"
    Medical Library Association Bulletin 56:235-67,
    380-403, 1968.

6. Richard H. Orr. "Measuring the Goodness of Library
    Services: A General Framework for Considering
    Quantitative Measure," Journal of Documentation
    29:315-31, 1973.

7. J. A. Urquhart and J. A. Schofield. "Measuring
    Readers' Failure at the Shelf in Three University
    Libraries," Journal of Documentation 28:233-41,
    1972.

8. C. H. Kim and I. M. Sexton. Books by Mail Service:
    A Conference Report. Terre Haute, Indiana State
    University, Department of Library Science, 1974,
    p. 8.

9. Ibid., p. 135.

10. Mary L. Bundy. Metropolitan Public Library Users.
    College Park, Md., University of Maryland, School
    of Library and Information Services, 1968, pp. 43-7.

11. Lowell A. Martin. Library Response to Urban Change;
     a Study of The Chicago Public Library. Chicago,
     American Library Association, 1969, pp. 208-9.

12. Lee Ash and Vernon R. Bruette. Interlibrary Request
     and Loan Transactions Among Medical Libraries of
     the Greater New York Area. New York, The Sur-
     vey of Medical Library Resources of Greater New
     York, 1966, p. 197.

13. Leonard Grundt. Efficient Patterns for Adequate Library
     Service in a Large City: A Survey of Boston. Ur-
     bana, Ill., University of Illinois, Graduate School of
     Library Science, 1968, p. 60.

14. Philip Morse. Library Effectiveness: A Systems Ap-
     proach. Cambridge, Mass., M.I.T. Press, 1968.

15. Nelson Associates, Inc. User Survey of the New York
     Public Library Research Libraries. New York,
     Nelson Associates, Inc., January, 1969, pp. III-7,
     III-29, D-32.

16. John A. Swets. "Information Retrieval Systems,"
     Science 141:245-50, 1963.

17. Michael D. Cooper. Evaluation of Information Retrieval
     Systems: A Simulation and Cost Approach.
     Berkeley, University of California, School of Li-
     brarianship, 1971, p. 35ff.

18. Different kinds of existing information retrieval systems
     can and should be compared to find relative merits.
     Three such systems were compared (punched card
     system, a handbook derived and printed from the
     punched cards, and the conventional library catalog)
     in a thesis by Norman D. Stevens, Comparative
     Study of Three Systems of Information Retrieval.
     New Brunswick, N.J., Rutgers University Press,
     1962, on input costs, output products and user's re-
     actions.

19. Ben-Ami Lipetz. "Catalog Use in a Large Research
     Library," Library Quarterly 42:129-39, 1972.

20. University of Chicago. Graduate Library School. Re-
     quirements Study for Future Catalogs, Progress

Report No. 2. Chicago, University of Chicago,
Graduate Library School, 1968, p. 13.

21. Elizabeth E. Duncan. Current Awareness and the
Chemist--A Study of the Use of CA Condensates by
Chemists. Metuchen, N.J., Scarecrow Press, 1972,
p. 80.

22. William J. Studer. "Computer-Based Selective Dissemination of Information (SDI) Service for Faculty
Using Library of Congress Machine-Readable Catalog (MARC) Records." (Unpublished Ph. D. dissertation) Graduate Library School, Indiana University,
1968, pp. 88-91.

23. Nelson Associates, op. cit., pp. III-27, III-30.

24. "Evaluating Reference Service," Synergy, No. 42, 1973,
p. 16.

25. Terry L. Weech. "Evaluation of Adult Reference Service," Library Trends 22:317, 1974.

26. George E. Rowland, et al. The Process of Professional Information Exchange Among Science Information Specialists. Washington, D. C., Clearinghouse
for Federal Science and Technical Information, U. S.
Department of Commerce, pp. 2-21, 2-22.

27. Bernard Vavrek. "The Nature of Reference Librarianship," RQ 13:216, 1974.

28. Terence Crowley and Thomas Childers. Information
Service in Public Libraries: Two Studies.
Metuchen, N.J., Scarecrow Press, 1971.

29. Charles A. Bunge. Professional Education and Reference Efficiency. Springfield, Illinois State Library,
1967.

30. Martin, op. cit., pp. 27-28.

31. Stanley McElderry. "Definition of Requirements for
Undergraduate Programs in University Libraries,"
in C. H. Kim et al., eds. Library Management:
Quantifying Goals. Terre Haute, Indiana State University, Department of Library Science, 1973,
p. 17-34.

INVENTORY

Henry Voos

> Up to thirty years ago it was common practice to
> inventory the entire book collection every two or
> three years by comparing the shelf list with the
> books on the shelves and with the "out" book cards
> in circulation trays. .... Today few public li-
> braries take regular, complete inventories, be-
> cause experience has shown that loss rates are
> low--and the cost of a complete inventory of a
> large or medium-size library is high.[1]

Introduction

It is debatable in the context of today's libraries in
society whether it is at all necessary or economical to inventory library collections. Costs of such inventories are
directly proportional to the size of the collections. The
frequency of inventory and its relationships to collection size
has concerned the library profession for many years. As
early as 1909, the American Library Association Committee
on Library Administration sent out a questionnaire on inventory frequency versus size of collection.[2]

In 1917, A. E. Bostwick lamented the fact that size
of libraries is a factor in frequency of inventory:

> The taking of inventory has become so onerous in
> large libraries that some are omitting it altogether,
> or taking it only at long intervals. This course
> seems indefensible in the case of the custodianship
> of public property.[3]

The American Library Association again surveyed libraries, including inventory practices, in 1927 and found that

TABLE I

Number of Libraries Inventorying Versus Collection Size, 1909

Collection Size	# Inventorying	# Non-Inventorying	% Non-Inv.
A (1,000-10,000)	29	6	17
B (10,000-50,000)	98	7	7
C (50,000-200,000)	34	3	8

TABLE II

Frequency of Inventory Versus Collection Size, 1909

Collection Size	6 mon.*	1 yr.**	2 yr.*	3 yr.*	5 yr.*	Irregular	% Inv. greater than 1 yr. int.
A	2	20	1	3	0	2	21
B	2	67	11	4	2	8	47
C	0	19	4	1	1	8	42

* 1 library about to lengthen period
** 1 library about to change to 2-year interval

annual inventories were taken by 25 per cent of libraries
having more than 100,000 volumes; 33 per cent of libraries
having between 50 and 100.000; 60 per cent of libraries
having between 20 and 50,000 volumes; and 70 per cent of
the libraries having a collection of less than 20,000.[4]

In the 1950's the Enoch Pratt Library (collection,
700,000+ vols.) took inventory after a lapse of 17 years and
concluded that inventories should be taken at least once
every ten years.[5]

In 1959, Ruth M. Baldwin sent 1,102 letters requesting information on inventorying practices, but received a non-
significant response. However, of the 56 college and university libraries replying, 43 per cent did not take any inventory.[6] She concluded that in the decision to inventory,

> Time and motion studies might be employed to
> actually determine the advisability of continuation
> or discontinuation of these practices (accessioning
> and inventory).

There are of course alternatives to an either/or decision on inventory, such as a progressive percentage being
inventoried each year, with the entire collection inventoried
in approximately a five-year cycle, or sampling the collections and inventorying only those sections which the sampling
shows to have many missing items, or just doing continuous
sampling over a period of time.

Justification

Central to the question of when and how to take inventory is that of why to take inventory. A small sampling
of the literature shows many of the reasons given.

A good general description is given by Reddy:

> The primary object of stock-taking is to ascertain
> the number of books missing during a particular
> period from the total stock as accounted for in the
> accession registers. The next object is to study
> the state of books, cleaning of the shelves, dis-
> covering the misplaced volumes and laying aside
> of books for examination as to their need of re-
> pairs, replacements and withdrawals. It is also

one of the objects to detect cases of vandalism and
to investigate the matter.   All the discrepancies
particularly in the shelf-list, accession register in
classification and cataloguing and in the charging
system, which escape the attention of the library
staff ordinarily, can be noticed while verifying the
stock and can be rectified. [8]

A similar statement was made by Hardin E. Smith,
who put certain of the reasons in perspective in terms of
priorities:

We did not consider some of the reasons often
given for taking inventory, such as reading the
shelves and weeding the collection; and filling
gaps in the collection was of only secondary importance. Keeping the catalog an accurate index
of the entire book collection we considered of utmost important in giving good library service.
A minor reason for taking an inventory is to
have an accurate statistical record of the library's
holdings. This information is of some little value
in comparing the library with others and in im-
pressing the taxing authorities and taxpayers with
the library's importance and performance (people
are impressed by statistics). [9]

Articles by Baldwin, Oxley, Russell ascribe to the
above reason. [10]   It is interesting to note that these same
justifications were also considered valid in China in 1937. [11]

D. O. Stine, a library trustee, adds the businessman's
comment:

Some merchants seldom, if ever, take an inventory
of their stock.   They are the small ones, the unsuccessful.   There are so many reasons why a
merchant should take frequent and regular account-
ings of his resources that the matter is not discussed.
It may be argued that a public library is a public service and not a business.   Is it not both? [12]

Another reason, which resembles the above, was given
by Bostwick when he related inventory to the "custodianship
of public property." [13]

Not everyone gives wholehearted approval to the taking
of inventory. The previously cited Wang article which justified inventory also stated that in a well-managed, well-ad-
ministered library inventories should be unnecessary.[14] A
more humorous look at inventory was taken by Dorothy Tunks
who, after setting up the staff and procedure to be followed
says that "one must maintain a respect for those whose initiative, constant devotion to duty, enthusiasm and plain stu-
pidity have made libraries what they are today."[15]

Methodology

The traditional method used in the nineteenth century
and still being used is described by Poole:

> Once a year, at least, the library should be
> thoroughly examined by comparing the books on the
> shelves with the shelf lists, noting every missing
> book, and later accounting for the absent volumes,
> so far as can be done. It was formerly the cus-
> tom to call in the books, and to close the library
> for two or three weeks while the examination was
> going on. The closing of the library is a serious
> inconvenience to the public, and is not necessary
> for the purpose of the examination. By going over
> the shelves while the books are in circulation,
> noting by shelf marks such volumes as are out,
> and repeating the examination several times at in-
> tervals of a week, the list of books not found will
> be greatly reduced. The binder's schedule and de-
> linquent list in the mean time will be examined,
> and finally the slips on which books not returned
> are charged.[16]

Another description, which more or less repeats the
1876 version of Poole is given by Rathbone:

> The usual way of taking the inventory is for two
> persons to work together, one reading the shelf-
> list, the other examining the shelves (in some li-
> braries the process is reversed, the reading being
> from the books on the shelves), a list being made
> of missing books by call number. In case of more
> than one copy of a book, the accession number is
> also read. After a session of reading, the missing
> books are looked for in the circulation records, at

the mending table, on the binder's lists, or among
books withdrawn for any of the library processes.
The shelves are re-read from these lists and each
subsequent step gone over several times.[17]

Although the foregoing methods are generally followed,
with minor variations, some other means are also used. One
of the fastest and most interesting techniques used is just
counting the volumes on the shelves and in circulation and
comparing these figures with the number of volumes in the
shelf-list.[18] The St. Louis Public Library did it this way
in 1917.[19]

The most modern method is, of course, one using the
computer to its fullest advantage. If both the shelf-list and
circulation file are in machine-readable form, much of the
labor used in checking can be eliminated:

Discussions with one of our systems engineers
produced a routine which put the shelflist on tape
(this was before our present circulation system
was installed. In fact, the taping of the shelflist
influenced the planning for the new circulation
routines), and the circulation records on another
tape. The computer then matched the tapes.
Cards which were not matched appeared on a printout listing--those from the circulation tape in one
column, those from the shelflist, a much longer
list, in another. It was then only necessary to
check the shelves for the nonmatches in the shelf-
list column....[20]

Photographic charging creates difficulties for inventorying. Enoch Pratt Library solved this as follows:

A routine was set up to handle the circulation records. The first week in May we began to remove
book cards from all books as they went into circulation. A card was placed in the book pocket reading: 'The book card has been removed from this
book temporarily for purposes of inventory.' ...
The books were charged photographically, but the
book cards were filed for the inventory check....[21]

An Australian library had a different approach to the
problem, as described by Lindsay Miller:

7. During the first week the stocktakers check the books on the shelves on the current stocktaking group.
8. During the next five weeks the books returned each day in this group remain on the appropriate shelves in the sorting room until checked by the stocktakers, preferably on a daily basis, with the shelf list. Books not in the group will, of course, be moved from the sorting room to the library several times daily.
9. All books returned overdue may be treated as ordinary returns if the overdue period is less than two weeks, as no overdue record will have been made regarding them.
10. All books returned overdue which have been overdue for two weeks or more and regardless of whether they belong to the current stocktaking group or not, should be checked daily, preferably by the stocktakers. The check of these books is in two parts:
   (a) The removal from the file of overdue records entries regarding them.
   (b) The sorting of them on to appropriate shelves in the sorting room.
11. After the completion of 10(b), the check outlines in 8 above should be made.
12. On the first morning of the sixth week the stocktakers check the overdue record with the shelf list. [22]

Sometimes libraries endeavor to come up with labor-saving techniques that may actually take longer. One high school library staff came up with the following:

The suggestion of a second set of charging cards in color came from two senior staff members. Taking inventory would consist of changing the cards--as simple as that! They volunteered to type the cards and the project was launched.
   Buff charging cards were made for each book the shelf list indicated was in our library at the last inventory. These were kept in charging files in the library office....
   The regular staff made two cards for all the new books and filed the buff ones with those being made from the shelf list....
   Routines fall into the following pattern with

selected student staff members working in pairs.
B handles the books, C the cards.
1. C reads the call number to B
2. B answers with the accession number
3. Cards are exchanged
4. B replaces the book (with the new card) on
   its fore edge.[23]

Another school library lists the items on pre-ruled
paper and then checks against the shelflist.[24] Florence Russell used a method that took much filing and refiling of records in order not to disturb service.[25]

Acceptable Loss Rates

Nowhere in the literature have we been able to determine what an acceptable loss rate might be. Logically
speaking, decisions in terms of whether one can replace
items, their intrinsic values, whether they are in or out-of-
print play an important part, as do factors such as which
part of the collection they are missing from. The literature
does show some of the decisions that have been made, but
has not provided a basis on which value judgments can be
made.

The Department of the Army until 1958 had in its
Regulations pertaining to Special Services libraries a 5 per
cent permissible loss. This was dropped in later versions
of the Army Regulations. The department of the Air Force
set up a sampling system and made permissible loss a function of the sample size, so that for a collection of 1500-
2500 titles, a sample of 241 was selected with 7 volumes a
permissible loss.[26] For collections varying between 1500
and 150,000 volumes, the permissible loss ranges between
3.0 and 2.8 per cent. A systematic sampling method is
recommended.

Enoch Pratt did an inventory in 1953, after a 17-year
moratorium and found only .3 per cent missing for each of
the 17 years.[27] Harvard found only a projected .5 per cent
of each collection to be missing.[28]

Irene Braden used sampling as a decision-making tool,
and stated that 5 per cent would be the cut-off point, and
therefore, if any part of the collection had more than 5 per
cent missing, it would be completely inventoried.[29]

A recent mimeographed report from the Santa Monica
Public Library, surveying the loss rates in thirty-one public
libraries, indicates that an average annual loss rate of .2
per cent to .5 per cent is most common (among those libraries that could give any figures).[30] A 5 per cent loss
was discovered over a period of 25 years in the East Chicago
Public Library.[31]

From the foregoing it is difficult to come up with a
valid permissible loss rate. A more detailed look at some
of the losses in libraries may help justify the use of sampling rather than complete inventories. It is highly probable
that different parts of a collection are used more or less
heavily depending on the user population, and on the changing
needs for information or recreation.

The Edmonton, Alberta Public Library inventories
biennially. After its 1962 inventory, it was questioned
whether the collection should be inventoried again in 1964:

> Any book inventory is a time-consuming and ex-
> pensive undertaking and librarians are frequently
> reluctant to get started when there are so many
> more immediate pressures on the staff. A survey
> of the literature indicated that most public libraries
> today do not do complete and regular inventories of
> their holdings. Most appear to avoid the matter
> entirely, simply replacing individual titles when
> they never seem to appear on the shelves, or they
> do spot checks. Based on what seemed to be the
> consensus of opinion, the Edmonton Public Library
> hoped to do the same, or at least place a wider
> space between its inventories.[32]

In toto, the Edmonton Public Library discovered 59
per cent of the adult collection and 41 per cent of the juvenile collection to be missing. This was analyzed by percentage missing versus branches, and found to vary between
1.90 per cent and 33 per cent of the collection. A range
this wide should raise some administrative questions.

An analysis by class and branch showed a range for
non-fiction as follows, in rank order:

TABLE III

% of Collection Missing in Rank Order[33]

Class	% of Total Missing
Canadian (Ref.)	.4
000	.7
400	1.2
200	2.1
Ref.	3.8
100	4.4
Foreign (Ref.)	5.1
500	6.6
300	9.4
800	10.1
700	12.9
600	19.0
900	24.3

We do not know what percentage of the entire collection each class represents.

With resources at a premium, a decision could be made from this data, plus density of collection by class, on what order to inventory in.

It was also interesting to note in this inventory, that although the total percentiles missing between adult and juvenile books were not significantly different, when examined on the basis of adult and juvenile fiction versus adult and juvenile non-fiction, a reverse pattern is found:

TABLE IV

Percentages of Adult and Juvenile
Fiction and Non-Fiction Missing[34]

	Adult	Juvenile
Fiction	36.31	67.42
Non-fiction	63.69	32.58

Braden, in her 1 per cent sampling also calculated the percentage missing by subject. These percentages varied between 1 per cent and 42.06 per cent.[35]

Emerson found the average annual loss rates for
classes 300 (2.1 per cent), 500 (3.9 per cent) and the 600s
(4.0 per cent).[36]

The inventory of the Niedersächsischen Staats- und
Universitäts-bibliothek at Göttingen found that the distribution
of losses in the various subject categories reflected the frequency of use of the collection.[37]

Unit Times

Varying unit time data can be calculated from the
available literature. Although not truly comparable, since
methods, layout, and personnel differ, the literature does
provide some ballpark ideas as to the possible cost of in-
ventory/volume if any of the methods are followed:

TABLE V

Unit Times for Inventory

Reference	Min. /Bk.
Brown & Strain (Automated)	0.716
Stebbins (Counting)	0.024
Bostwick	0.026
Sivertz	1.008
Sanner	0.825
Smith	0.952

Conclusions

The literature shows that although it is expensive and
time-consuming, sometimes there is a rationale for inventorying. The methodologies used would tend to indicate that
sampling methods can show which parts of the collection
should be inventoried. Studies by students at Rutgers Graduate School of Library Service have shown that systematic
sampling, if the shelf-list method is used, is the most cost
effective sampling method.

Notes

1. J. L. Wheeler and Herbert Goldhor. Practical Administration of Public Libraries. N.Y., Harper, 1962, p. 476.

2. Corinne Bacon, Svla Wagner and H. C. Wellman. "Report of the Committee on Library Administration," American Library Association Bulletin 3:207-8, 1909.

3. A. E. Bostwick. "A New Kind of Inventory," Library Journal 42:369-71, 1917.

4. American Library Association. A Survey of Libraries in the United States. Chicago, 1927. v.4, p. 119-32; "Frequency of Inventory," Library Journal 52: 827-8, 1927.

5. Marian Sanner. "Pratt Takes Inventory," Journal of Cataloging and Classification 11:125-32, 1955.

6. R. M. Baldwin. "Library Journal's Survey of Accession & Inventory Practices," Library Journal 84: 1048-52, 1959.

7. Ibid., p. 1051.

8. P. Konda Reddy. "Stock-Taking of Libraries," in All-India Library Conference, Fifth. Proceedings. Indian Library Association, 1942, p. 150.

9. H. E. Smith. "Taking Inventory," Library Journal 87: 2847, 1962.

10. Baldwin op. cit., p. 1052; B. H. Oxley. "Inventory Solitaire," Wilson Library Bulletin 27:647-8, 659, 1953; Florence Russell. "The Sunday Inventory," Library Journal 57:704-5, 1932.

11. Y. Wang. "How to Take Inventory," Wen-hua T'u-shu-kuan-hsüeh Chuan-k'o Hsüeh-hsiao Chi-k'an 9:9-12, 1937.

12. D. O. Stine. "The Library Inventory," Wisconsin Library Bulletin 19:424, 1923.

13. Bostwick, op. cit., p. 369.

14. Wang. op. cit., p. 9.

15. Dorothy Tunks. "Instructions for Stocktaking," Assistant Librarian 49:18, February 1956.

16. W. F. Poole. "The Organization and Management of Public Libraries," in U. S. Dept. of the Interior. Bureau of Education. Public Libraries in the United States of America.... Washington, U. S. G. P. O., 1876, Part I, p. 504.

17. Josephine A. Rathbone. Shelf Department. Chicago, A. L. A., 1930, p. 5.

18. H. L. Stebbins. "Counting a Library," Library Journal 47:715-6, 1922.

19. Bostwick, op. cit.

20. N. A. Brown and Paula M. Strain. "Use of an Automated Shelflist," Sci-Tech News 21:37, 1967.

21. Marian Sanner. "Pratt Takes Inventory," Journal of Cataloging and Classification 11:126, 1955.

22. Lindsay Miller. "Stocktaking in Lending Libraries," The Australian Library Journal 5:66, 1956.

23. Elizabeth G. Scott. "Taking Inventory with Double Charging Cards," Mountain Plains Library Quarterly 8:8, Fall 1963.

24. Cordelia Smith. "The School Library Inventory," Wilson Library Bulletin 6:208-9, 1931.

25. Florence Russell. "The Sunday Inventory," Library Journal 57:704-5, 1932.

26. U. S. Dept. of the Air Force. Air Force Library Service. Washington, 22 March 1965. (Air Force Regulation no. 212-1) pp. 16-7.

27. Sanner, op. cit., pp. 125-32.

28. R. H. Moody. "An Inventory at Widener," Harvard Library Bulletin 2:130-1, 1948.

29. Irene A. Braden. "Pilot Inventory of Library Holdings,"
     A. L. A. Bulletin 62:1129-31, 1968.

30. W. L. Emerson. "The Problem of Inventory," Cali-
     fornia Librarian 23:156, 1962.

31. H. E. Smith. "Taking Inventory," Library Journal
     87:2847-8, 1962.

32. "The Biennial Book Inventory," Edmonton Public Li-
     brary. News Notes 9:80, 1964.

33. Ibid., p. 48.

34. Ibid., p. 81.

35. Braden, op. cit., p. 1130.

36. Emerson, op. cit., p. 156.

37. Hartwig Lohse. "Die Lesesaalrevision der Niedersäch-
     sischen Staats- und Universitätsbibliothek Gottingen,"
     Zeitschrift für Bibliotherswesen und Bibliographie
     7:141, 1960 (#2).

PART IV

THEORY AND PHILOSOPHIES

THEORIES OF INFORMATION

Susan Artandi

At a general level information may be looked upon as a means to ensure that changing societies make wise decisions. Information is sought about society as it is now, and about the ways in which it is changing, to find out what alternatives to present practices exist or can be found. We hope for "well informed" decision-makers who will evaluate information in terms of society's goals and needs in the process of allocating resources.[1] This implies such things as the desirability of having information, the idea that information can favorably affect human behavior, and that it can be obtained, communicated, and utilized in the process of achieving human goals. Information science as a discipline assumes that information can be scientifically studied, analyzed, and controlled for its improved utilization at all levels.

Problems related to the utilization of the increased information output of today's society can be fully appreciated when one considers the fact that man's intellectual capacity has been substantially constant and finite on the time-scale of civilized society. Contrasted with this is the need to function in a sophisticated industrial environment in which the complexity of information increases at an even faster rate than its volume; the result is a gradual degradation of our relative intellectual capacity to deal with information.[2]

The concept of information is ambiguous, complex, and difficult to separate from such other concepts as communication and meaning. The words "information" and "information flow" have been used as labels for an amorphous mass of ill-defined activities and phenomena such as sets of linguistic expressions, changes in the state of knowledge of recipients, the number of natural language lexical units ut-

157

uttered or written per second, the accession rate of new documents, or any other rates associated with any process involved in message transfer.[3]

Compared to the extensive studies in the field of mathematical communication theory, relatively little theoretical work has been done relating to information in these and similar contexts. Since a considerable part of the information that we deal with individually or collectively as a society is communicated through human (natural) language, limitations inherent in language represent a major source of imprecision in the information transfer process. Success in communication depends to a great extent on the choice of words of the writer or speaker and the meaning of these words to the reader or listener. When we speak to one another or when we communicate in writing we do not transmit our thoughts, we do not transmit words as linguistic entities; we transmit physical embodiments of words. Thus, when discussing the concept of meaning outside of the strict bounds of logic or mathematics and in terms of everyday human thought and conversation, the meaning of meaning turns out to be a rather ambiguous concept. Colin Cherry warns us that to speak of utterances and their meaning is almost to make a dualism like body and soul. Meaning is not "a label tied around the neck of a word or a phrase but it is more like the beauty of a complexion which lies altogether in the eye of its beholder (but changes with the light)."[4]

Communication is a process of adjusting understandings and attitudes, of making them congruent or of ascertaining how and where they disagree. Implicit in the process are a common language, a common interest, and some degree of common understanding. Similarly, meaning can exist only through what we have in common in our lives, minds and language.[5]

In this essay the concept of information is considered within the framework of two major theories--Shannon's Mathematical Theory of Communication, and semiotics, the study of signs and sign systems--to see how they can contribute to the better understanding of information as we deal with this concept in the context of information systems.

The Mathematical Theory of Communication

Shannon carefully defined the boundaries of the

Mathematical Theory of Communication when he stated that

> The fundamental problem of communication is that
> of reproducing at one point exactly or approximately
> the message selected at another point. Frequently
> the messages have meaning; that is they refer to
> or are correlated according to some system with
> some physical or conceptual entities. These se-
> mantic aspects of communication are irrelevant to
> the engineering problem. The significant aspect is
> that the actual message is one selected from a set
> of possible messages. [6]

Thus the word information in Shannon's theory is used in a
special sense that must not be confused with its conventional
usage; in particular, information must not be confused with
meaning. In the context of the Mathematical Theory of Communication, two messages, one with meaning and one which
is meaningless, can be exactly equivalent in terms of information. The word information relates not so much to what
you do say but what you could say, and applies not to individual messages (as the concept of meaning would) but to the
situation as a whole.

The boundaries of what Shannon calls the engineering
problem are further clarified by Weaver[7] when he outlines
three levels of communication problems: the technical (engineering) problem, the semantic problem, and the effectiveness problem.

The technical problem is concerned with the accuracy
of transference from sender to receiver of such things as a
finite set of symbols (written or speech), a continuously varying signal (telephonic or radio transmission of voice or music), or a continuously varying two-dimensional pattern (television).

The semantic problem relates to the identity or close
approximation in the interpretation of meaning by the receiver
as compared with the intended meaning of the sender. Complex problems are involved that can be reduced to tolerable
size but can not be completely eliminated. The explanations
used are never more than close approximations of the ideas
being explained but they are understandable because they are
expressed in language which previously has been made reasonably clear through operational means.

The problem of effectiveness concerns the effect of

the message on conduct, conduct defined very broadly. Psychological and emotional aspects are involved as well as value judgments which are necessary to give useful meaning to words.

Since information in the context of Shannon's theory is a measure of one's freedom of choice when one selects a message, the amount of information (entropy) in the simplest cases is measured by the logarithm to the base 2 of the number of available choices. Thus, the two-choice situation (log $2=1$) has unit information or 1 bit of information. More realistic cases are those when an information source makes a sequence of choices from some set of elementary symbols and the selection is governed by probabilities which are not independent but which at any stage of the process depend upon preceding choices (Markoff processes).

When an individual selects letters from the alphabet to construct a message in English, probabilities are involved that relate to the English language. For example, the probability is zero that an initial j will be followed by b, c, d, f, g, j, k, l, q, r, t, v, w, x, z. In these situations the amount of information (entropy) is defined through the amount of freedom one has in constructing messages. Maximum entropy is the freedom of choice one would have with the same set of symbols if there were no restrictions, and information is low in situations that are highly organized and are not characterized by a high degree of randomness. Given a fixed number of choices, information (entropy) is largest when all probabilities are equal and information is small when one event has a very high probability. When the actual value of entropy is compared to maximum entropy we refer to the relative entropy of the source. One minus relative entropy is called redundancy and it is that fraction of the message which is determined by the accepted statistical rules governing the use of the symbols in question. Part of a message is redundant in the sense that if it were missing the message would be essentially complete. For example, the fact that the redundancy of English is about 50 per cent means that half of the letters and words we use are under our free choice and half are controlled by the statistical properties of the language.

In Shannon's model of a communication system (Figure 1) the <u>information source</u> selects the <u>message</u> out of a set of possible messages. The transmitter changes the message to produce a <u>signal</u> that is suitable for transmission over a

Susan Artandi   161

| Information Source | Transmitter | Signal | Received Signal | Receiver | Destination |

Message   Noise   Message
                                 Source

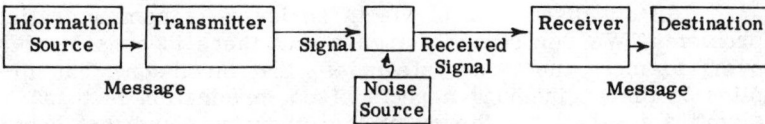

Figure 1. Shannon's schematic diagram of a general
           communication system.

communication channel from the transmitter to the receiver.
The receiver reconstructs the transmitted signal into a message and forwards it to the destination. In this process,
ideally the transmitted signal would be identical with the received signal. However, during transmission (or at one of
the terminals) noise or unwanted distortions and errors occur and create a change in the transmitted signal. Implicit
in this model are such concepts as information, channel capacity, coding methods, noise, and the characteristics of the
signals being transmitted.

        In such a communication system the information source
and the message destination are usually human beings. For
example, a human being types a message on a teletypewriter
in the form of letters and spaces. The teletypewriter serves
as a transmitter that encodes each character as a sequence
of electrical pulses. The pulses are transmitted by a pair
of wires to another teletypewriter that acts as a receiver and
prints out the letters and spaces to be read by another human being.

        As the signals travel from one teletypewriter to the
other an intermittent connection or an extraneous current may
create noise by altering some of the signals. As a result
the teletypewriter that serves as receiver may print some
wrong characters and cause the received message to differ
from the transmitted message.

        In telephone communication the transmitter is a set of
devices which change the sound pressure of voice into a varying electrical current. The channel is the wire, and the receiver a set of devices that change the varying electrical
current back into sound.

General Applicability of Shannon's Theory

In his discussion of the three levels of communication
problems, Weaver strongly argues that there is considerable
overlap among the three categories, that the theory that applies to the engineering aspects of communication is to a
significant extent the theory of the other two, and that separation into three levels is artificial and undesirable. The semantic and effectiveness problems can only be solved if the
signals are transferred accurately, which means that while
the semantic and effectiveness problems are irrelevant to the
engineering problems, the engineering problems are not irrelevant to the other two. The semantic problem is inter-
related with the effectiveness problem and taken together they
contain most, if not all, of the philosophical content of the
general problem of communication.

When considering the more general applicability of
Shannon's model Weaver suggests that the original model
should be modified to take into consideration the semantic
problems involved in communication. In his modified diagram (Figure 2) a box labelled semantic noise is inserted
between the information source and the transmitter and the
box which was originally labelled noise is now labelled
engineering noise. Weaver calls semantic noise the distortions of meaning or the ambiguities not intended by the information source which nevertheless affect destination. A
semantic receiver is interposed between the receiver and the
destination to subject the message to a second decoding to
match the statistical semantic characteristics of the message
to the statistical semantic capacities of the audience one
wishes to affect. An extended theory would also take into

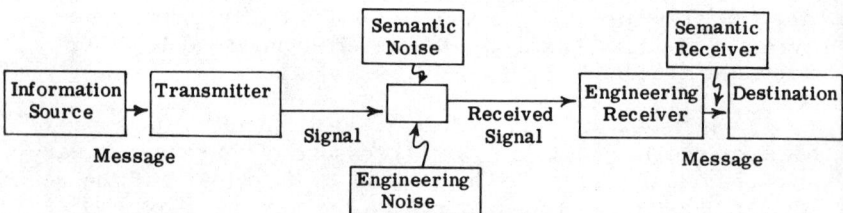

Figure 2. Weaver's modified diagram of a general communication system.

consideration not only the capacity of the channel but also the capacity of the destination. By direct analogy to channel overload which results in reduced fidelity, overcrowding of the capacity of the audience creates error and confusion.

The relevance of the engineering aspects of communication to the semantic and effectiveness aspects in terms of the need for the accurate transference of signals is quite evident, and it is reasonable to believe that Shannon's model of a communication system can serve as a useful point of departure for extended thinking about information problems. Some confusion seems to arise, however, when an attempt is made to draw a parallel between Shannon's measure of information (entropy) and the concept of information in its conventional sense.

Fairthorne feels that much confusion in the literature seems to result from the "superficial study and purely rhetorical extrapolation of Shannon's strictly delimited Information Theory beyond its valid scope."[8] He points out that Shannon considered explicitly the most reduced activity that still retained the essentials of communication: the activity of devising patterns of signals appropriate to a physical mode of communication in order to indicate choices made from a particular set of messages. While this involves informing in the sense of signalling, the recipient is only told which message has been chosen but he is not told what the message is or what it refers to, if anything. Nor is there any guarantee that even if he is told and even if he could interpret the code, the recipient would be informed in the sense of change of state in his knowledge. For these reasons Shannon's model describes only certain aspects of signalling and neglects to indicate who signals to whom about what.

Cherry seems to think along similar lines when he explains that information of some kind or other certainly seems to be a concept of value in many fields but this does not say that one mathematical theory and one measure have indiscriminate application. The Shannon measure of information was set up for a specific purpose and concerns the signals themselves. What these signals mean, or what their value or truth is, simply cannot be discussed in the language or communication theory.

Bar-Hillel warns us that impatient scientists in various fields have applied the terminology and the theorems of the statistical communication theory to fields in which the

term information is used in a semantic sense or in a pragmatic sense. [9]

The application of the terminology of the Mathematical
Theory of Communication to characterize various organizational situations may or may not be appropriate, depending
perhaps on how far the analogies are carried. It has been
suggested that a complex management situation can be characterized by a large entropy value and that low entropy systems are those in which the manager needs to consider the
impact of relatively immediate events about which he knows
a great deal. Entropy can also be thought of as the measure
of the absolute complexity of a management information system, while redundancy measures the relative safeguards and
controls built into the system. [10]

Semiotics

Since all communication proceeds by means of signs
and all information is carried by a vehicle such as a signal,
a sign, or a symbol, it is reasonable to suggest that semiotics, the general science of signs and sign systems, should
furnish an important framework for the study and analysis of
information phenomena.

In semiotic terms the elements of human language are
signs, sounds or written marks produced by members of a
group in order to be perceived by other members and to influence their behavior. The usage of a set of signs is determined by syntactical, semantical and pragmatical rules which
correspond to the three levels of semiotics presented sche-
matically by Cherry as successive abstractions.

Syntactics is the study of signs and the relation between signs. It concerns the physical signs only, abstracted
from their users. Semantics is concerned with the study of
relations between signs and their designata, independent of
specific communication events. Semantic information can be
regarded as information conveyed by sentences "in the language" and not information to and from a particular person.
Semantics is interested only in the study of meaning for standard interpreters in standard conditions. Pragmatics is the
study of signs in relation to their users. It is the most in-
clusive level of study and includes all personal and psychological factors as well as questions of value and usefulness
of messages.

Nauta[11] divides the study of information and semiotics
somewhat differently into two broad approaches, the transmissional and the meta-approach, connected with potential
and actual information respectively. Metasemiotic information presupposes linguistic information or at least some device for grammatical symbol organization.

Pragmatic information is the richest articulation of
information and finds its fullest realization in human communication.

Transmissional information is the poorest representation of information and transmissional theory is the most
general approach to information in that it abstracts from the
concrete semiotic situation and reduces communication to its
most elementary aspects. It is the most simplified, the
most abstract approach and, therefore, has the most general
applicability.

Cherry places Shannon's information theory in the
field of syntactics while Nauta strongly emphasizes the distinction between transmissional and syntactic information.
Nauta believes that the presentation of Shannon's transmissional theory of information as a theory of syntactic information is "perhaps the most serious misconception ever made
in the field of information theory."[12]

Nauta argues that Shannon's theory has been called
syntactic because of the practice of identifying syntactics
with abstraction of meaning. Syntactics is, however, related to meaning, and syntactic information theory is much
more complicated than Shannon's theory of communication
engineering and signal transmission. While many of the
theoretical aspects of meaning are reflected implicitly in the
statistical properties which are studied by transmission
theory, to view language communication as a finite-state
Markoff process is unsatisfactory. Syntactics is related to
meaning and syntactic information is inherent in linguistic
information because of the hybrid nature of language.

The Hybridity of Human Language

Human languages show hybridity in the sense that they
represent a transition between natural and artificial language.
Human language is natural because it is learned and developed
within the language community concerned. The naturalness

of human language is characterized by the facts that: 1) the
meaning of words is not tied up once and for all, but goes
through a certain development, not arbitrarily determined be-
forehand, and 2) the rules of language are "de facto" rules
instead of "de jure" rules.

Human language, however, also has an artificial side
because the "de facto" rules are crossed by "de jure" rules,
particularly the rules of grammar and semantic rules, and
because it is regulated by consciously chosen cultural con-
ventions. Therefore human language has its place between
the natural language of signals and signs and the artificial
language of logic. Or, to put it differently, human language
may be placed between two ideal models of language:
1) where the whole language as well as its future development is controlled by "de jure" rules, and 2) where there
is no regulating of the language whatsoever and only the
factual functioning of the language, which goes through perpetual development, is involved.

This view of human language can be used to characterize index languages* and their use in document surroga-
tion.

Index languages are artificial in the sense that the
rules of the language are "de jure" rules and the development of the language is (more or less) controlled and regulated. In indexing the content of a document which is described in a hybrid, natural language is "translated" into
an artificial index language. As equivalencies of meaning
are sought the words of the artificial language which were
established by "de jure" rules are interpreted and re-inter-
preted in terms of the semantic and pragmatic information
contained in the natural language text of the document. In
this process the effective functioning of the index language
tends to be closely tied to the understanding of the "de facto"
development of the natural language involved.

Pragmatic Information

The essence of man's position is that he must decide
in the face of uncertainty, namely, in the face of uncertainties

*The term "index languages" is used here in a broad sense
to include languages involved in classification systems, subject headings, indexing systems, etc.

relevant to his everchanging purposeful state. Nauta defines pragmatic information as that which reduces these uncertainties.

Looking at the problem from a purely quantitative point of view, decision theory should be an excellent tool for dealing with rational decisions in the face of uncertainty. The situation is more complex, however, because pragmatic information is directly related to human values, not only economic but ethical and aesthetic values, and to human experiences in a very broad sense of the word.

If we accept the proposition that pragmatic information is that which reduces uncertainty, this implies that the greater the amount of information the less should be the uncertainty, or, conversely, greater uncertainty means less information. There is a logical opposition between uncertainty and removal of uncertainty that can cause difficulties in differentiating between the meaning of pragmatic information as a means of removing uncertainty and the meaning of information (entropy) in the context of Shannon's theory. In the latter case information is a measure of uncertainty, and the greater the uncertainty the greater the amount of information. To clarify this seeming contradiction Nauta suggests that what we deal with in Shannon's theory is potential information (information capacities), and what is measured is the amount of information that can be communicated, not the amount that is actually communicated.

Whittemore and Yovits[13] suggest that pragmatic information can be measured in terms of its observable effects, more specifically in terms of its effect on the decision state of the decision-maker. They define decision state as the complete description of the decision-maker's overall level of understanding about a particular decision situation at a particular point in time.

The proposed quantitative measure is time- and decision-maker-oriented since it assumes that the same information will have different significance to different decision-makers at any time or to the same decision-maker at different times.

Nauta's definition of pragmatic information has some interesting qualitative implications. To reduce uncertainty information must be relevant in the sense that it can be integrated and evaluated in terms of the individual's prior

experiences (his existing state) and his possible future states
and activities. This suggests that that information which is
not relevant or not new (is known by the individual) is not
information since neither is capable of reducing the state of
uncertainty of the individual, while negative information is
in fact information. A message on nuclear magnetic reso-
nance received by a layman, for example, is not information
with respect to him because he lacks the prior experience
which would allow him to evaluate the message and his uncertainty is not reduced.

The proposition that information is always determined
relative to the interpreter, his actual internal state and organization, allows us to consider indexing as an activity
whose purpose is to provide information to an interpreter of
whose ever-changing purposeful state the indexer has only a
minimal, generalized, and frequently static model.

In the process of indexing the indexer has the dual
role of acting as an interpreter on his own behalf and in
terms of the purposeful state of his model of the future
readers of the document. Since the author did not write for
the indexer but for the reader, close similarity among the
indexer as an interpreter, his model of the reader, and the
author's model of the reader should help to increase the
chance for effective communication in a document retrieval
system. [14]

Summary

It can be reasonably argued that both the Mathematical
Theory of Communication and semiotics contribute significantly
to the better understanding of information as we deal with
this concept in the context of information systems. While
the engineering aspects of communication are important because of the need for the accurate transference of signals,
it is clear that it is the semantic and effectiveness problems
of communication and the nature of semantic and pragmatic
information that should be the foci of future studies.

Shannon's model of a communication system suggests
that it can be used as a point of departure for extended
thinking about information problems in general. When dealing with Shannon's measure of information (entropy), however, we must guard against unsubstantiated and purely spec-
ulative extrapolation of the Mathematical Theory of Communication beyond its valid scope.

The logical opposition between uncertainty and removal
of uncertainty can make it difficult to differentiate between
the meaning of information in its conventional sense and the
meaning of information in the context of Shannon's theory.
In the former case information is regarded as a means of
removing uncertainty; in the latter, information (entropy) is
a measure of uncertainty.

The understanding of the hybrid nature of human languages provides some insights into the characteristics of index languages and the indexing process. The view that information is always determined relative to the interpreter,
his actual internal state and organization, allows us to reexamine the communication problems involved in indexing.

Notes

1. Edward L. Brady and Lewis M. Branscomb. "Information in a Changing Society," Science 173:961-6, 1972.

2. J. Lukasiewicz. "The Ignorance Explosion: a Contribution to the Study of Confrontation of Man with the
Complexity of Science-based Society and Environment,"
Transactions of the New York Academy of Sciences,
1972, pp. 373-91.

3. Robert A. Fairthorne. "Morphology of 'Information
Flow'," Journal of the Association of Computing
Machinery 14:710-19, 1967.

4. Colin Cherry. On Human Communication. 2d ed.
Cambridge, Mass., M.I.T. Press, 1957, p. 117.

5. John B. Pierce. "Communication," Scientific American
227:31-41, September 1972.

6. Claude E. Shannon. "The Mathematical Theory of Com-
munication," in Claude E. Shannon and Warren
Weaver, The Mathematical Theory of Communication.
Urbana, Ill., University of Illinois Press, 1949, p. 31.

7. Warren Weaver. "Recent Contributions to the Mathematical Theory of Communication," Ibid., pp. 95-117.

8. Fairthorne, op. cit., p. 711.

9. Cherry, op. cit., p. 222.

10. Martin K. Starr. Management: a Modern Approach.
     N.Y., Harcourt Brace, 1971.

11. Doede Nauta, Jr. The Meaning of Information. The
     Hague, Mouton, 1972.

12. Ibid., p. 203.

13. Bruce J. Whittemore and Marshall C. Yovits. "A Gen-
     eralized Conceptual Development for the Analysis and
     Flow of Information," Journal of the American So-
     ciety for Information Science 24:221-31, 1973.

14. Susan Artandi. "Information Concepts and Their Utility,"
     Journal of the American Society for Information
     Science 24:242-5, 1973.

COOPERATION LIMITED

Leonard Grundt

When Ralph Shaw was inaugurated as President of the American Library Association in 1956, he said to his fellow librarians: "Our basic task, regardless of the kinds of libraries in which we work, deals with books for people; including all kinds of people, in all the various shadings of their needs."[1] Public, school, academic, and special libraries constitute but one type of social institution serving human needs for information, education, recreation, etc. They are primarily vehicles for the collection, preservation, dissemination, and use of recorded knowledge in whatever forms it may exist--from stone tablets to computerized data bases; and when knowledge is not recorded, they may play an active role in producing media.

Supplying society's needs for recorded knowledge is an enormous task that cannot be performed by any single library or other social agency. What is required is the coordination of independent activities resulting from the organization of combinations of libraries and other institutions. John Mackenzie Cory of the New York Public Library, drawing upon the "generation" concept used to describe stages in the development of computers, has identified four generations of library organization, as follows:

1. The first generation of library organization is limited to a single library of a single type (e.g., public, college, school, or special). It may be independent or it may be an auxiliary part of a larger, non-library parent organization.
2. The second generation consists of a system, network, or combination of several libraries, all of the same type (e.g., a public library system,

171

a university departmental library system, a school
library system, or a special library system).
3. The third generation is a combination of
several different types of libraries, whether independent or dependent (e. g. , METRO [one of nine
reference and research library resources systems
in New York]).
4. A possible fourth generation, still largely
to be developed, is a combination of various types
of libraries and of non-library agencies concerned
with related activities (e. g. , information retrieval
and transfer, culture and recreation, or conserva-
tion and exhibition). 2

Cory's four generations represent increasing levels of
library cooperation. Libraries have been working together--
to some extent--for more than a century. Professional publications are replete with essays advocating and describing
joint projects. A reader of the literature can easily conclude that cooperation is one of the guiding principles of library service. Its benefits have been stated many times:
more effective and more efficient use of collections, staff,
and physical facilities; improved access to collections;
elimination of unnecessary duplication of collections, staff,
and physical facilities; improved public services; and possible reductions in operating expenditures and capital expenditures.

Cooperative programs have included the following activities: planning (e. g. , the regional medical library program and state plans for library systems); collection development (e. g. , Public Law 480 and the Farmington Plan);
shared cataloging (e. g. , the Anglo-American Cataloging
Rules and Library of Congress printed card service); centralized processing (e. g. , the Colorado Academic Libraries
Book Processing Center and the Nassau Library System in
Garden City, New York); shared bibliographic access (e. g. ,
the Rocky Mountain Bibliographic Center and the Pacific
Northwest Bibliographic Center); union catalogs and lists
(e. g. , the National Union Catalog and the Union List of Se-
rials); joint storage of collections (e. g. , the Center for
Research Libraries and the Associated Colleges of the Mid-
west); interlibrary loan (e. g. , the NYSILL network in New
York and similar programs in other states); telecommunica-
tions (e. g. , facsimile transmission and teletype networks);
joint computer use (e. g. , the MEDLINE program and the
Ohio College Library Center); extension of use privileges

(e.g., statewide library cards and the open access program
of State University of New York libraries); cooperative reference centers (e.g., the Bay Area Reference Center in San
Francisco and the Metropolitan Reference and Research Library Agency in New York City); cooperatively-sponsored
learning centers (e.g., the Philadelphia Student Library Resource Requirements Project and degree programs offered
by academic institutions at public libraries); combining libraries (e.g., the Joint University Libraries in Nashville,
Tennessee, and the school-public library system in Hawaii);
and collaborative staff development (e.g., the Western Interstate Commission for Higher Education workshops and the
continuing education programs of local professional associations).

     The foregoing enumeration is by no means complete,
but it does demonstrate that there are many ways in which
libraries can work together as well as with related organizations. Yet, while nearly all librarians have given lip-service
to sharing resources, the facts show that professionals do
not always practice what they preach, as Richard M. Dougherty pointed out in a 1972 Library Journal article.[3] Although there have been some successful cooperative ventures,
most joint programs in the library field have failed. Why?
Let us examine some of the barriers to working together.

     The major obstacle seems to be psychological; there
is a distinct ambivalence toward cooperation among those
who operate libraries. Every librarian faces a conflict between bolstering his own library and bolstering libraries in
general. This dilemma is analogous to the problem of striking a balance between the welfare of the individual and that
of society at large. It is a matter that cannot easily be re-
solved. The Advisory Committee on Planning for the Academic Libraries of New York State, headed by David Kaser,
made the following observations:

          ... Success or failure of an inter-library effort is
     largely determined by the degree to which conflict-
     ing concepts of accountability for the participants
     are or are not inherent in the project. Every li-
     brarian feels two kinds of responsibility to the
     books under his oversight. First, he must hus-
     band them as part of the chattel of the institution
     by which he is employed--of the institution that
     bought and paid for them and stored them in many
     cases over generations. Second, he must view

them as part of the general intellectual heritage of
mankind which he ought somehow to make available
to all men. Cooperative projects which call for
him to fulfill the latter responsibility while violat-
ing his stewardship to the former responsibility
seem certain to fail. Faced with such a dilemma,
he must surely perform first in the best interest
of the institution that employs him and writes his
paycheck. 4

Consequently, cooperation works only as long as each
librarian views the arrangement as beneficial to his institution and to himself. In our culture, the concerns for self-
preservation, self-sufficiency, autonomy, individualism, and
freedom are paramount. Attempts to abridge a person's
"inalienable rights" to "life, liberty, and the pursuit of hap-
piness" are met with great resistance. Once library coop-
eratives, systems, consortia, networks, councils, federa-
tions, and associations are perceived by the participants as
threats to their independence and integrity, the attempts at
collaboration are doomed. But the coordinating organization
may continue existing anyway, in name only, because it is
considered unprofessional not to support cooperative programs.

It is very difficult for anyone to admit publicly his
opposition to collaborative ventures. Therefore, a librarian's
resistance to change will often not be openly expressed in
emotional terms but rather in intellectual ones. For example, instead of saying he fears centralization of technical
services, a librarian may speak of centralized services not
serving the individual needs of users adequately. Quite un-
derstandably, many joint projects are viewed as threats to
job security and professional status. Programs such as
planning for statewide or regional library services, sharing
bibliographic access, compiling union catalogs and lists,
storing collections cooperatively, facilitating interlibrary
loan services, and agreeing upon reciprocal user privileges
tend to succeed far more easily than efforts to effect centralized selection, acquisition, cataloging, and processing of
materials or to combine libraries of the same type or of
different types. This happens because centralization of functions and integration of libraries may result in shifting of
positions or even reductions in employment, while the other
collaborative ventures would have less impact upon staff.
In general, programs developed to expand access to collections and services will be accepted with fewer objections

than projects designed to increase the operating efficiency of
libraries. They may indeed be welcomed because they create
new job opportunities. Furthermore, "The more a cooperative affects a library's local policies and procedures, the
less the likelihood that the cooperation will be viewed with
enthusiasm."5

  While the attitudes of librarians can cause a program
to succeed or fail, they are by no means the only factors to
be considered. The parent bodies of libraries frequently
serve as stumbling blocks to cooperation. By their actions,
governments, hospitals, schools, universities, businesses,
professional associations, and other corporate bodies can
make joint efforts involving their libraries difficult if not impossible; sometimes with good reason, but as often without.
For example, the U. S. Department of Agriculture requires
that the library at its Plum Island Animal Disease Labora-
tory in New York not send any books to other libraries since
there is a possibility of spreading infection; only photocopies
are made available to others. Many commercial organizations limit public access to their offices and libraries because of space limitations, staff limitations and fear of having their trade secrets pirated by competitors. It is not
uncommon for academic institutions, especially those under
private auspices, to restrict the use of their libraries to
members of their campus communities due to financial considerations; outsiders may often only use the libraries
after paying special fees. Moreover, as is the case in Nassau County, New York, local ordinances can prevent the
transfer or sale of library materials from public institutions
to other libraries, even if the items to be discarded are no
longer of use to county agencies and are of potential value
to others; excess books must be declared surplus property
and sold as waste paper to the highest bidder.

  The residents of a community can serve as a barrier
to collective action if they oppose joint ventures between
their local library and neighboring public libraries or if they
vote against the merger of their library with others, even
in a situation where local taxes might be lowered as a result of decreased costs. Every town seems to want a public
library it can call its own, even if a large regional library
located within a thirty-minute drive--possibly supplemented
by small branches, bookmobiles, or a books-by-mail ser-
vice--would prove to be more effective and efficient.

  It is not always the fault of librarians that cooperative

acquisitions programs involving colleges and universities fail
to develop very useful collection development policies.   On
this matter, the Advisory Committee on Planning for the
Academic Libraries of New York has wisely stated:

> The uniform experience of libraries everywhere
> and in all ages has been that if they attempt to
> rationalize their collecting efforts cooperatively
> before, rather than after, interinstitutional ration-
> alization of curricula, they are likely to be inef-
> fective.   This is true because librarians determine
> only in a very superficial sense what goes into
> their collections.   Often they do select the individ-
> ual titles to be gotten and identify those to be fore-
> gone, but they make these selections within param-
> eters not determined by themselves but settled
> upon by faculty and administration in the normal
> process of academic decisionmaking.   Rather than
> making such broad policy decisions in this regard,
> librarians in effect implement the decision of others.
> Librarians are aware that they appear, to an un-
> fortunate degree sometimes, to duplicate among
> themselves expensive resources and services;   but
> they also know from long experience that books go
> where the professors are, and that if there are
> two professors in the State or even in the same
> city who are teaching in the same subject area,
> however narrow, their libraries will be forced to
> duplicate resources.   Eliminate one man or the
> other, or put them both at the same institution,
> and the aggregate library cost will be halved.   Such
> decisions as these, however, are not librarians' to
> make. [6]

In these times, cost considerations frequently militate
against cooperative programs.   For example, interlibrary
loans have been predicated on a reciprocal relationship between libraries.   However, the strongest libraries tend to
be the heaviest lenders and the weakest libraries the heaviest
borrowers.   The costs of the interlibrary loan system have
been borne principally by the largest libraries.   They cannot continue to assist smaller institutions without either being reimbursed for sharing materials by the federal or state
governments or charging borrowers fees for this service.
The availability of federal and state funding--particularly
during the last decade--made much coordination of library
activities possible, but the future does not look too promising.

Historical and geographical factors also affect the way libraries collaborate. If libraries have competed with each other over a long period of time, it is not likely that they will suddenly begin to work cooperatively. Sharing requires trust--and trust does not develop overnight. With respect to geography, let it be said, to use an old cliché, out of sight is out of mind. If libraries are not close to each other physically, or if good communication and transportation linkages between them do not exist, they are not apt to engage in successful joint programs.

Finally, a word about copyright as a barrier to collaboration. Until now, the "fair use" doctrine has seemed to give libraries relative freedom to reproduce copies of materials in their collections for scholarly purposes. Such consortia as the newly-formed Research Libraries Group (consisting of the Research Libraries of the New York Public Library and the libraries of Harvard, Yale, and Columbia) are planning cooperative acquisitions programs involving the purchase of only single copies of expensive publications and the subsequent reciprocal sharing of these research items by means of photocopying and other communications techniques. Proposed changes in the copyright law as well as future Supreme Court decisions may forbid any reproduction of copyrighted materials without payment of fees. Such legislative and/or judicial action could seriously impede the practice of interlibrary loan and the development of library consortia.

So much for the obstacles to cooperation. What should be done to enhance it? I believe the federal and state governments will have to play a more active role in providing money for research and experimentation to determine the most effective techniques for achieving cooperation among libraries and between libraries and related agencies. Funds should also be made available for reimbursing the larger institutions that absorb an inordinate share of the costs of joint programs.

It is important to move away from the current emphasis on standards for specific types of libraries. Instead, standards should be formulated for measuring the extent to which the total library resources of various geographical areas are coordinated. How well regional or statewide cooperative arrangements satisfy the needs of the population in a given area for recorded knowledge should be of greater significance than the size of an individual library's

collections, staff, physical facilities, or budget. In line
with this concept, the organizations responsible for accredit-
ing educational institutions should evaluate them on the basis
of the availability of library services to their faculties and
students--regardless of which libraries furnish these ser-
vices--rather than on the basis of whether or not the schools
have adequate libraries themselves. If a new college is
started next door to a well-established public library, it is
far better to have the public library supply the needs of the
academic community than to develop a library at the school
ab initio.

There will be greater cooperation only when librarians
and society at large have a mutual commitment to work together for the benefit of all people. We must somehow
change the attitudes of those who see little value in sharing.
Joint programs must be perceived not as potential threats
but as potential promises of more effective and more efficient library services. When that day comes, we will have
reached Cory's "fourth generation" of library organization
and development.

Notes

1. Ralph R. Shaw. "Inaugural Address," ALA Bulletin
   50:492, 1956.

2. John Mackenzie Cory. "The Network in a Major Metropolitan Center (METRO, New York)," Library Quarterly 39:91-2, 1969.

3. Richard M. Dougherty. "The Paradoxes of Library
   Cooperation," Library Journal 97:1767-70, 1972.

4. New York State Education Department. Report of the
   Advisory Committee on Planning for the Academic
   Libraries of New York State. Albany, 1973, p. 3.

5. Dougherty, op. cit., p. 1769.

6. New York State Education Department, op. cit., p. 6.

PUBLIC AND TECHNICAL LIBRARY SERVICES:
A REVISED RELATIONSHIP

Doralyn J. Hickey

Among Ralph Shaw's regular admonitions to his students was a sentence which soon became a refrain: "Don't do efficiently something which shouldn't be done at all." Even after the student had heard that imperative countless times, it still had some shock value, for it commanded innovative thinking. In the student's mind, it came to signify the precise opposite of continuing a procedure "because it's always been done that way." It went beyond the idea of perpetual questioning of the status quo toward the concept of revolutionary readjustment.

It is in this spirit of revolutionary readjustment that the library world needs to face the question of the relationship between public and technical services in its institutions. The literature is replete with "how I run my library good" articles describing ways in which to reorganize acquisitions and cataloging routines to make them more effective. Little serious attention has been paid to the matter of whether there should be a "technical services" unit existing separately from a "public services" unit in the library. There have been some oblique challenges to this separation of powers: the University of Nebraska's "dual assignment" as described by Frank Lundy and Kay Renfro;[1] the development of the "bibliographer-specialist" as studied recently by Eldred Smith;[2] and the use of the special library model of total service to the client as a prototype for all of librarianship.[3] In each case, however, caveats have been entered to show that the fundamental pattern of separation of technical from public services has not truly been altered. Nebraska, for example, moved its professionals from one divisional administration to another in order to achieve a dual work experience; it did not obliterate the lines between divisions. The

subject specialists whom Smith encountered operated, more
often than not, as transcenders of the library order rather
than reuniters of it as they moved back and forth among departments in response to the needs of their clientele. The
special library model of client-centered information services
is regularly envied but at the same time eschewed by the
staff of other types of libraries who understand this model
to be applicable only to small, compact libraries.

Since much effort has been expended to "make more
efficient something which perhaps should not be done at all,"
it seems desirable to raise anew the question of whether the
time-honored division between technical and public services
in libraries ought to be retained and improved in its functioning, or whether, on the other hand, new types of divisions
ought to be constructed. The conservatives and pessimists
will undoubtedly protest that the creation of new patterns is
an academic dream, not a viable alternative, for old and
complex institutional structures are not easily transformed.
This objection, however realistic and well taken, will be ignored in this analysis, in favor of another Shavian dictum,
"Think big."

In order to facilitate some "big thinking," a few elements of common sense about the user's approach to the library ought to be mentioned. The library user does not
understand and does not, in general, care to understand the
organizational structure of the library system; he wants the
library to perform on his behalf without much effort on his
part. This has been termed the "black box" syndrome. To
the library's clients, the input is the user's request, the
output is the desired material or information, and the library
serves as a mysterious black box which somehow transforms
the input into the output. How this magic is accomplished
is of interest primarily to other magicians, not to the audience. The user thus cannot be expected to understand why
he is required to enter the black box itself upon occasion in
order to try to make it perform its magic; nor is he likely
to be able to distinguish clearly between the public-library
black box and the academic-library black box. Any black
box of the library type ought to do the job, and the closer
at hand it is, the better.

The conclusion of this argument must be that the library's clientele becomes knowledgeable about the structure
of the system only when forced to do so. Ideally, the client
should be able to make his request known and have it filled

without interruption. Most libraries do not, however, operate this way. The client is expected to know what type of
library will best fit his needs, to know which staff levels
will best be able to respond to his needs, and to know the
procedures according to which his needs will be met. It is
not unusual, for example, to hear a reference librarian tell
a client that he/she cannot obtain the needed material because "it is being recataloged"; or to hear a circulation assistant tell a user that the material is "not here yet but it's
'on order';" or to see a patron standing puzzled before a
catalog card on which is stamped, "For further information,
see main entry." The final insult comes when the client
learns that no one in the library seems to be able to find
the material which he/she wants, even though the material
has been purchased, ostensibly for the client's benefit. The
client may legitimately wonder whether he/she should be contributing his/her hard-earned pay toward the support of such
an ineffective system.

     Suppose, then, that someone at a cosmic level in li-
brarianship took seriously the patron's lament and set about
to rearrange the library to suit its clients. What would hap-
pen? In order to answer this question, the most common
client needs must be laid out and new systems projected to
meet them. For the sake of argument, consider the most
frequent patrons' requests and relate them to the current organizational structure:

     1) "Do you have ... ?" A seemingly reasonable ex-
pectation of a client is that a library be able to supply specific materials which the patron knows to have been published. That expectation is directed toward the public service sector of the library which in turn can only respond by
redirecting the question to the technical services sector in
which the materials are purchased, received, made available, and recorded. The resultant subquestions--e.g. "Can
I see it?" and "Where is it?" and "Where can I buy a copy
of it?" and "Why don't you have it?"--likewise involve the
total library staff structure in one way or another. If the
public service sector is unable to deliver the material or
the requisite information about it, the technical service sector is likely to receive the blame, whether deserved or not.
It should probably be noted that the size of the library varies
in direct proportion to the degree of blame accorded to technical services (or vice versa, for no one seems to know
whether one causes the other), but the fact that a library is
small does not seem to assure that the technical services

staff will be excused from that blame. Even in a one-person
library, there is a tendency to charge the other "self" (the
cataloging self) with the responsibility by saying, for example, "Well, I just haven't had time to catalog that yet."

2) What do you have on ... ?" This expectation presumes the existence of approaches to materials by means of
topics, concepts, ideas, or forms. Again the question is
normally directed to a public service librarian who must
then quiz the records provided by the technical services librarians in order to answer it. The subquestions here may
be "What do I look under?" "Don't you have anything else?"
"How do I find what I want in all this stuff?" "Don't you
have anything on it at all?" Some of these requests clearly
expect value judgments as well as the simple provision of
bibliographic guidance; such judgments would normally be
made within the public service sector, but it must be recognized that the way in which materials are organized for use
involves the projection of value decisions by the technical
services staff with which the public services librarians must
be familiar. All too often, this is not the case, and the
user once again cannot be assured that the functioning of the
library system operates to his advantage.

3) "Can you help me please?" This question tends
to focus the demand upon public services, depending upon
what follows. If the next phrase is "I'm not sure what I
want," then the public service staff must elicit the context
of the request and try to match the library's resources to
it. Obviously this means utilization of technical services as
well. If the phrase is "Maybe if I could just look around,"
the user is making a bid to rely upon the organizational
skill of the technical services librarian, but the wisdom of
the procedure must be assessed by public services staff.
The phrases "You see, I've got this problem" or "I need
some advice" often serve as a prelude to long and complex
negotiations which depend upon the skill of the public service sector and the prescience of the technical service group
for success.

It appears reasonably clear that the naiveté of the
user's approach to the library demands from the library
staff a group of services which transcends the division between public and technical functions. If the patron were,
on the other hand, to try to serve himself in this kind of
situation, he might find himself unable to make this system
of complex interrelationships work. What, then, can the

typical library client expect in response to his questions?
One answer is "Learn the system." The problem with this
solution is that even those who designed the system often
cannot fully exploit it, with all of their knowledge of its
workings gained over years of experience. How can a neo-
phyte be expected to do what the expert cannot do? Another
answer is, "Tell us more precisely what you want." But
this may be exactly what the patron cannot do, else he would
already have done it. "Trust us" and "Come back in a little
while." Here the user is told, in effect, that the staff cannot produce what he wants under the demands of the moment
but can eventually come up with something, even if it is a
substitute, that may be satisfactory. The degree to which
such a response is believable depends upon the client's prior
experience with the system and the general credibility of the
library. The final response, "No one's perfect," admits de-
feat and acknowledges that the system has outwitted even
those who design, maintain, and monitor it.

        The library's clientele thus may quite often find itself
out of phase with the organizational structure of the library.
The library services are designed to move materials through
the system and onto storage shelves, there to be interpreted
by a group of people who have had little or nothing to do
with the procedures which put the materials into storage.
Yet the user presents what seems to him simple and reasonable requests: "Do you have this?" "What do you have on
this topic?" "Can you help me with this problem?" The librarian responds, in effect, "I can help you learn whether
we have it, find works on a subject, or analyze your problem, but only if the total library system is working well;
for what I can do for you depends on whether other people
have been doing their jobs." To the library's patron, this
is a "cop out" answer. In his eyes, the library has, by
opening its doors, implicitly contracted with him to provide
a service; the fact that the public services librarian does
not understand how the system can be manipulated to the
patron's benefit is, in effect, a breach of contract.

        A fairly obvious solution to such a dilemma is to re-
orient the library's systems around the concept of direct
and effective service to the clientele. What currently exists
is an orientation toward indirect service to the clientele. If
any direct service is involved, it is apparently aimed at the
preservation and storage of materials rather than the solution of user's problems. Thus the library might creatively
consider whether its services could become client-centered

rather than materials-centered. In other words, if librarians
take seriously the responsibility to focus upon user needs,
they might be forced toward a totally different pattern of
work organization.

For the sake of argument, consider a structure of library services based upon the three basic questions which
the library clientele most often voices, namely: 1) "Do you
have this?" 2) "What do you have on this topic?" 3) "Can
you help me with this problem?" How might such a structure behave?

In order to respond to the user's initial--and in the
case of the specialist client, probably the most frequent--
question, the library would present him with a rapid and accurate means of determining whether the local collection
could produce the needed material. The assumption here is
that the patron has something in the way of a specific citation to the desired item and that he can reasonably be expected to recognize a matching citation in the library's files.
Meeting this patron's requirement would entail the development of a staff whose job it is to produce a "finding list"
designed to respond quickly to queries involving "known
items." Such a list would not be, it should be noted, exclusively oriented toward what is now called descriptive cataloging, for "known item" approaches may involve what is
currently called subject cataloging when the name of a person or group is the topic of the material required. The
finding list would thus provide an index to all names associated with a work (with the requisite variant forms of those
names included), all titles of works (with variant titles, if
appropriate), all series designations, and some "form" designations (in those cases in which a physical feature of the
work makes it outstanding, e.g. , it has a fore-edge painting).

There is some question as to whether the finding list
should be produced on a strictly local basis, through a combination of local and regional efforts, on a regional basis,
on a national basis, or in varying combinations of local, regional, and national efforts. Obviously, the use of computer
facilities, very likely in an on-line mode, would be entailed
by such a plan. In fact, the development of a data base
such as that of the Ohio College Library Center lends itself
very well to the production of such a finding list. If this
data base were then coupled to a local or regional circulation control module, the library user could query the finding
list at whatever location suited him and determine where the

"known item" could be located most effectively.   In any
event, the local library would have a staff unit devoted to
the entering of new materials into the finding list, adjusting
the list, and assisting users with problems in the manipula-
tion of the list. Such an organization would transcend the
current division between public and technical services in
which the cataloger lists the materials, the circulation attendant maintains records of its whereabouts, and the reference
staff tries to interpret the list to the public.

The library user's second question ("What do you
have on this topic?") must be divided into subquestions in
order to devise a strategy for meeting this need.   If the
topic turns out to be a name, then the finding list may solve
the problem;   if, on the other hand, the topic is vague and
imprecise, the client may require a reference counseling
service.   Since the user's question is capable of a variety of
interpretations, the library's organizational structure ought
first to respond by providing a "screening" service.   Although there are a number of people who envision that such
a service can be offered successfully by means of an on-line
computer console with an extensively indexed data bank, it
would seem more desirable--and more humane--to provide
the user with a human interpreter to do the initial screening.
This person would be skilled in interpersonal communication
and knowledgeable in the field of search strategy and bibliographical control systems.   He would be responsible for determining whether the client requires general tutelage on
bibliographic patterns, an introductory guide to a subject
field of interest, the provision of specific pieces of information, or a more detailed bibliographic counseling service.
Depending on the judgment of this staff member, the user
would be channeled into one of several service areas: a) a
section in which library staff assists clients in completing
an appropriate programmed learning sequence to discover
the basic principles of bibliographic searching in various
broad disciplines, e.g., how to approach the location of materials in the physical sciences; b) a section in which are
located subject specialists and various published guides to
the literature of specific fields, possibly building on the
"Pathfinder" approach already used in reference work;   or
c) an information service section in which the library staff
would field the user's question and produce the requisite
answer for him.   The bibliographic counseling service would
be set up separately to deal with those patrons whose needs
are either too imprecisely verbalized or so highly complex
as to require extended discussion and perhaps a trial-and-
error approach.

It is not particularly difficult to envision the planning and preparation necessary to implement the three administrative sections enumerated here. The "programmed learning" section would involve staff in the preparation of such sequences, the monitoring of their success, and discussion of the process with the clientele. The emphasis would be upon effective search strategy, not upon the location of specific materials within the library's collection. General bibliographic knowledge rather than a high degree of subject specialization would be the most desirable characteristic of the staff in that section.

The section in which subject specialty would be stressed entails the amassing of a collection of subject guides to the literature of various fields, the indexing of these guides for quick retrieval (possibly indexing on characteristics such as the level of sophistication which a particular guide presumes), and the preparation of mini-bibliographies to meet specific recurring subject needs. In addition, the staff would have to be sufficiently expert in various subject fields to be able to advise their clients upon both the size of the materials base likely to be unearthed by their questions and the general quality of the literature in the field.

The "quick information" section would be staffed with fast thinking, creative people, noted for their ability to perceive the import of a question and draw together the needed expertise from among the subject specialists as required, and to produce a fast, adequate summary of the data needed by the client. In this section of the library, the user might well be furnished with browsing material for his amusement until such time as the answer to his question is secured. For lengthy or complex questions, the staff member might suggest that the user return at a specified time, telephone for the information later, or have the information transcribed and mailed to him. It is conceivable that staff in the "quick information" section might alternate assignments with the subject specialist group, since the information unit would be expected to operate effectively under a great deal of pressure and might need to trade off assignments in order to continue to provide a high level of information service.

The bibliographic or reference "counseling" service would be established to meet the needs of the patron whose ability to focus upon his own problem is limited or whose area of interest is too complex to fit neatly into the subject

specialties offered regularly by the library. This unit would
be designed to deal with the third type of user question ("Can
you help me with this problem?"), whether the question be
initially verbalized that way or turn out to be of that type
even though verbalized as "What do you have on this topic?"
There might be some question as to whether this unit should
be subsumed administratively under the type two service, so
that all patrons who do not have a clearcut "finding list"
problem would be sent through a "screening" process first
and subsequently referred to bibliographic counseling if necessary. In some ways, however, it might be more effective to establish bibliographic counseling as a separate division, primarily because its function would be to discuss with
the client, on a one-to-one personal basis, the nature of his
problem and the various alternative solutions envisioned. In
a sense, this unit would be the "reassurance" section of the
library, functioning basically to relieve the fears of patrons
who need help but are either afraid to ask for it or are so
out-of-step with the library's subject organizational pattern
as to find no home in the library's service structure. The
staff in this unit would be skilled in interpersonal counseling
techniques and be knowledgeable in general about the bibliographic systems in various fields. The counselor's role is
seen here as one in which he personally guides the client
through the library's structure, manipulating it for the client
and leaving him on his own only when the client indicates
his ability to function effectively without further help.

In all of this description of new library service structures, nothing has been said about the traditional acquisitions,
cataloging, classification, processing, and circulation functions. Of these "traditions," some would remain, though
probably transmuted and placed largely in the hands of support staff. Certainly the materials would still continue to
be purchased or otherwise obtained for the collection; thus
some acquisitions functions would remain. Materials would
have to be stored for retrieval, thus necessitating a processing function. It is likely, however, that the arrangement of
materials by a relative classification scheme would be discarded, although a relative subject order for the guides in
the subject specialty section would probably by maintained.
For the bulk of the collection, shelving by size and date of
receipt could become the norm. Maintenance of circulation
records would certainly be necessary, as would the control
of special forms of materials such as individual issues of
periodicals. Materials handling would be streamlined, with
emphasis always upon speed and accuracy of record-keeping;

the use of mechanical and electronic devices for repetitive
operations would be maximized.

It is, of course, conceivable that a new division between public and technical services could emerge, that is,
between those who acquire, process, and circulate the materials, and those who deal directly with the library's clientele. This is a risk which librarians enamored of the structure here described may be willing to run; nonetheless, the
materials-oriented systems which would underlie the client-
centered services would have to be geared carefully to the
support of the client, not to the convenience of the staff. If
this delicate balance is to be protected, a supervisory staff
of system-monitors would probably have to be developed. It
remains to be tested as to whether such a newly designed
structure could avoid the pitfalls of the present one, but perhaps it at least has a better chance of doing so.

It should be noted that such a drastic revision in library structure entails consequences which are difficult to
comprehend. The expected response from most librarians
is "Yes, that's an interesting idea, but ..." There are, of
course, many partial solutions to the current split between
public and technical services which are not so drastic. Some
have already been mentioned: dual assignments and subject
specialists, for example. Others are currently being tried:
the task force approach to problem areas, involving committees using both public and technical services personnel;
departmentalization of all services relating to certain disciplines, to provide "cradle to grave" care of materials in
various subject fields; and rotation of personnel in a kind
of local internship approach, so that staff will get the "feel"
of problems in other divisions of the library. A projected
solution which seems not yet to have been attempted is the
establishment of one or more "ombudsman" posts between
public and technical services. These representatives of the
library as a whole, and of its patrons, would seek to diag-
nose trouble spots and project needed investigatory action to
eliminate them, as well as to negotiate interpersonal relationship solutions. Certainly if a totally new structure is
inconceivable, an intermediate measure of the ombudsman-
type could be a decided asset.

    Perhaps it is an overexaggeration to assert that the
division between public and technical services has progressed,
especially in large libraries, to the point of no return, at
least under present organizational patterns. Yet the anger

and hostility which are so often vented by one toward the other--or are vented to an outsider who happens to be available to listen to the complaints--are perceived to be at such a height as to demand drastic action. If the basic philosophy of librarianship is to match materials with the needs of people, then it seems clear that a more client-oriented structure of library service is required.

Notes

1. Frank A. Lundy. "Dual Assignment: Cataloging and Reference," Library Resources & Technical Services 3:167-88, 1959.

2. Eldred Smith. "Academic Status for College and University Librarians--Problems and Prospects," College & Research Libraries 31:7-13, 1970.

3. Ada Winifred Johns. Special Libraries. Metuchen, N.J., Scarecrow Press, 1968.

BEYOND THE PROMISES OF AUTOMATION

Norman D. Stevens

> So let us think kindly of those who would frighten
> us by slogans and catch-words about the great and
> growing mass of the world's literature, and of
> those who would take pity upon our benighted state
> to solve all of our problems with machines they
> have not yet thought about.[1]

Ralph Shaw was a practical person, especially when
it came to the application of machines for library purposes.
His practicality was born of considerable experience in the
development and use of machines for such purposes, including the invention of--among others--the Rapid Selector, and
of an analytical mind which led him to examine closely other
machine applications. When Jesse Shera used the quotation
from Shaw that I have used above as a preface to an article,
he commented that, "reread today, after the passing of almost fifteen years, Shaw's pronouncements, like those of
Pythia, read as a curious mixture of wisdom, triviality,
error and even charlatanry."[2] Shaw, of course, was quick
to respond by pointing out that Shera's examples, real and
imagined, of achievements, "paint a distorted picture of
what this means to operations of libraries and information
services, currently, or for the next decade for that matter."[3]

Other clashes of this kind between Shaw and the more
vocal proponents of automation were frequent. He strongly
felt that the age of complete automation of libraries was not
imminent and he was not hesitant to express that view. So
strongly did he express those views that many have felt that
he was somehow unalterably opposed to the use of machines.
Wasserman's assessment of his role, however, is more
valid: "Ralph Shaw, even when cautioning against the ex-
travagance of some of the claims made for mechanization,

has demonstrated by his own professional contributions, first
as a library administrator, and later as a library educator,
a high degree of responsible leadership in advancing the
cause of technological progress in librarianship."[4]

One of Shaw's most skillful examinations of the topic
of library automation was in a paper that he presented to the
20th annual conference of the University of Chicago Graduate
Library School on the Future of the Book; Implications of
the Newer Developments in Communication. In that paper,
which was "a discussion ... [of] the parts of library work
which we have come to consider conventional and the ways
in which they may be affected by the newly evolving technology,"[5] Shaw summarized his thoughts about "the probable
impact of mechanization, as applied to operations within the
library itself":

> 1. By and large, library services are related to
> a mode of use which is relatively leisurely and con-
> templative as compared with the comparatively fre-
> netic requirements of switching gear, computations,
> mass communications, and so-called 'documenta-
> tion problems.' With this in mind and with the
> need to keep tools in balance with the entirety of
> an operation, it does not appear likely that the
> types of use made of most libraries would gain
> much by large-scale mechanization of services or
> that mechanization of services would do much to
> facilitate the predominating types of use.

> 2. Library services, as distinguished from mass
> communications and the so-called 'documentation'
> services, do not lend themselves to standardization,
> are not adequately repetitive for automation, and
> are not likely to exist in sufficient volume in the
> generality of libraries for the machine to serve as
> more than a minor aid for the next generation at
> least.

> 3. There appears to be no probability that any of
> the mechanical or electronic devices available or
> in sight will replace the book as a means for stor-
> ing, retrieving, and presenting the type of ma-
> terials normally stored and serviced by libraries.

> 4. Some of the new devices offer limited promise
> in the field of routines and techniques in the larger

libraries, but only the simplest and least costly of
these appear to have offered any promise of general applicability in libraries. [6]

After almost twenty years, the continuing relevance
and the lasting validity of Shaw's basic conclusions, especially those relating to the future of the book, are remarkable. Our experience since 1955 allows us to supplement
Shaw's thinking and suggests some additional reasons why
total automation of the library, with all of its implications,
is only slightly closer today than it was then.

The newly evolving technology of the 1950s is, in
many cases, still newly evolving. Its development has not
progressed as rapidly as expected. Shaw critically analyzed
the early experiments with telefacsimile transmission. He
pointed out that while the text of Gone with the Wind had
been transmitted from one place to another in a matter of
seconds, the common error of citing only part of the operation as the total operation meant that all of the necessary
and attendant steps, and the time they required, had not been
properly taken into account. "A slow messenger could have
hobbled from the hotel from which the transmission was
made, to the Coolidge Auditorium, where the reception took
place, stopping for a game of tiddly-winks, and still have
delivered the book in half the total elapsed time or less."[7]
As anyone who has recently experimented with the use of
telefacsimile transmission can testify, Shaw's slow messenger, twenty years older and even slower, could easily re-
peat his feat today.

Shaw also pointed out that a machine that cost much
over $1,000 would be economically useful only to a few hun-
dred libraries. While the actual dollar figure might be
somewhat higher today, the library market is still not sufficiently large to warrant special attention by equipment manufacturers. Even equipment that should be inexpensive and
which would have widespread applicability is not produced
solely for the library market. As early as its annual report for 1958 the Council on Library Resources described
the need for and the anticipated development of the cataloger's
camera. While the need for such a camera still exists, its
development, despite funding for it from the Council on Library Resources, no longer is realistically discussed. Instead, one continues to find in the literature descriptions of
how-I-built-my-own-almost-but-not-quite-the-same-cataloger's-
camera-good. Larger equipment intended for other markets

must be adapted and modified to meet library needs.   Under
these conditions the use of technology by libraries can only
progress slowly.

Human difficulties have been, and continue to be,
another major stumbling block to the achievement of the
promises of the new technology.   In many cases librarians
simply lack the ability to clearly understand and analyze
even their simplest problems despite the teaching of Shaw
and many others.   An example, appreciated by Shaw, is that
of a major American academic library whose systems staff
concluded that they could not consider the development of an
automated circulation system which might require the insertion of a book card and pocket in each book.   Since the library did not previously have book cards and pockets in its
book, to add them, it was concluded, would require an enormous and costly increase in the shelving space required for
the collections.   This would be true if a book card and
pocket were measured and the measurement was multiplied
by the number of books in the collection.   Quite obviously,
however, measuring a book before and after insertion of a
book card and pocket would indicate that inserting something
that thin into a book does not increase its size in any measurable way.   In addition, either the squeezing together of
books on a crowded shelf or the amount of space left at the
end of a shelf for growth in the collections would readily ac-
commodate the minute change that might occur.   In any case
the net result would not be a substantial increase in the total amount of shelving required.   If we cannot analyze our
problems any more sensibly than that, we can hardly expect
to improve our operations, even by the use of machines.

Unfortunately the human problem goes beyond that
fundamental weakness of the quality of staff.   A diversity of
research and development into the use of technology in libraries is good, for there is not necessarily only one correct way to do an operation and, even if there were, experimentation by a variety of libraries or networks would be useful in seeking to arrive at the most efficient way.   But development is often done locally more for reasons of pride
than of logic;   and a frequent major stumbling block to the
development of effective cooperative efforts in the use of
automated systems is the achievement of effective administrative and interpersonal relationships on a continuing basis.
Under those conditions, then, clearly human difficulties
stand in the way of real progress.

Costs, which Shaw touched on in part, remain the largest piece of the problem. We continue to have a large number of dreamers who describe in glowing terms what the new technology might mean in the way of large-scale changes in library operations. While it is still "Just as well to admit at the outset that whatever one man can dream, sooner or later another man can build,"[8] the costs of doing so must be considered. Some large-scale systems have been designed and built. If they are actually operational it is likely to be within the companies that manufacture them, such as IBM's Los Gatos operation, or in specialized high-priority contexts, such as the U. S. Army Missile Command's use of the Magnavox "Magnavue" system. In either case costs are not likely to be adequately taken into account. Others have developed and presented what they maintain are realistic plans for the large-scale use of technology in more normal situations and have, in some cases, even attempted to implement such plans. One of the best known of these has been the Massachusetts Institute of Technology's Intrex project, which was initially defined in detail at a Planning Conference on Information Transfer Experiments in 1965.[9] Although apparently unsuccessful, MIT has attempted to put those plans into operation in an effort, primarily supported with money from the Council on Library Resources and not from the MIT library operating budget, to bring about a major change in library services there. As early as 1970, however, Overhage, one of the chief planners of Intrex, recognized that the dreams of Intrex were not going to be realized by 1975. Speaking at a Conference on Collaborative Library Systems Development, he indicated that,

> In the past, my stance on this issue has been like this: We are talking about a new mode of access to information resources which may be sufficiently powerful to constitute an entirely new way of doing intellectual work.... Computers are expensive, but they have enabled men to extend their intellectual reach and to deal successfully with problems that had previously defeated them by their complexity. If it becomes clear that a similar extension of intellectual power can be provided by future library technology, then--I used to say--the necessary budgets will be forthcoming.
>
> Well, I still think that eventually the money will be found. But, ladies and gentlemen, this is November 1970. Most of our great libraries are

in deep budgetary trouble, our universities are
struggling with unprecedented deficits, and our national priorities are directed away from intellectual
goals. In such a situation, experimentation can
and should continue; at least one node of the future network should be established at a major library and its operation studied; but I can no
longer escape the conclusion that the large-scale
introduction of new technology into our libraries
will have to wait, no matter how powerful a mode
of access it can provide.[10]

The budgetary outlook within universities and their
libraries did change substantially between 1965 and 1970 and
it has not improved much, if any, since 1970. The earlier
expectation of change, however, was unrealistic, even within
the more favorable budgetary climate of the 1960s. Until
libraries can demonstrate, on a step-by-step basis, the
realities and not just the promises of the new technology,
and can show those responsible for the basic financial decisions what change will mean, it is unlikely that a drastic
reallocation of resources, of the kind required by Intrex and
other projects, will take place. Gradual change in the percentage of available funds assigned to the library would seem
to be the most that could be hoped for. An analysis of the
possible budgetary impact of Intrex on MIT, as presented in
the planning report, may help to clarify this.

Project Intrex will, of course, result in an increased emphasis on libraries at MIT; and we
can reasonably expect to see an increase in the
relative size of the MIT library compared to other
universities (it has been declining steadily since
1930). With due allowance for all these factors,
we might expect the total amount of stored information in the MIT information-transfer system of
1975 to be more than ten times as large as it is
in the library of today. We conclude that the magnitude of the information available in 1975 could
demand a 15-fold increase in the budget of the library. While the advances sparked by Project
Intrex could result in a decrease in the actual budget, a more probable outcome, if past experience
is any guide, will be a very great increase in the
services rendered. Thus we might expect that the
total budget for information transfer service at
MIT will be of the order of $15 M in 1975.[11]

In the past decade the relative position of the MIT library has declined further. In 1964/1965 the MIT library was 39th (of 64 academic libraries in the Association of Research Libraries) in total volumes, 33rd in volumes added, and 44th in total operating expenses. At the end of 1973/1974 the MIT library was then 44th (of 82 academic libraries in the Association of Research Libraries) in total volumes, 44th in volumes added, and 61st in total operating expenses. MIT's library collections, if they are considered to be the equivalent of the total amount of stored information in the MIT information-transfer system, have grown from 959,212 volumes to 1,527,594 volumes and by 1974/1975 should total about 1,650,000 volumes. Although a substantial increase, that is still a long way from being ten times as large. The MIT library's total operating budget has grown from $1,003,942 in 1964/1965 to $2,533,774 in 1973/1974, which does not approach a 15-fold increase. It seems likely that its budget might be more nearly $3 M in 1975 than $15 M.[12]

The promises of automation were there, and what might be done was well described. The planners, however, seemed to have had an essentially unrealistic attitude about the importance of the library and information in the academic community and, therefore, of the possibility of being able to increase its importance over a relatively short period of time. At MIT, as elsewhere, the library has been fortunate to secure 3-4 per cent of the institution's total educational and general budget. To expect major reallocation of resources to the extent that the library at MIT, for example, in ten years might receive almost 10 per cent of the institution's total educational and general budget was unrealistic. As libraries seek to make use of the new technology it is going to take longer to do so, if to do so is indeed dependent upon receiving a larger share of the pie. Libraries simply cannot expect the kind of major reallocation of resources that would be required to bring about dramatic changes in a short period of time.

Despite all of those problems technology continues to have a significant impact on library development. Despite the flights of fancy of those who feel that "library computerization has about three years left, during which either joint-sharing or mini-computers will prove beyond a doubt the economic necessity of the computer, or it will go,"[13] a return to "the little library ... where the librarian charged out books by hand on brown paper squares torn from kraft bags"[14] hardly seems likely.

As Shaw indicated, "Library routines, techniques, and services are now mechanized to some extent. The question is not whether we will mechanize but rather at what level of sophistication we will find ourselves ten or twenty years from now."[15] That is only slightly different from Shera's conclusion that, "the mechanization of the library, and the emerging information science that it rests upon, are not transitory enthusiasms. Librarians are confronted by a movement that has been steadily developing over the past thirty years and already has some impressive achievements to its credit. Librarianship is not going to be untouched by the machine."[16] The intervening years have validated those conclusions as well. The most recent of those writing on this general topic continue to conclude that, "Despite a few critical responses to the threats of technology, its alleged misuse, or its failure thus far to produce significant operating economics, the research library community has accepted, with varying degrees of knowledge or enthusiasm, the need for some basic changes in library procedures and operations, including more effective use of technology. However, the view that there may need to be even more basic conceptual and operational changes in the ways that libraries function and provide access to recorded knowledge has perhaps not yet been generally accepted by the library or the scholarly communities."[17]

It is now almost twenty years beyond 1955 and only ten years from 1984 and the promises of automation still lie ahead. The time scale no longer seems important. We tend to exist, after, all in a continuum, not in an either/or, today/tomorrow situation. The use of technology for library and information services has existed for some time and continues to grow and expand. By 1984 libraries will be making greater use of technology than they are today, and by 2004 greater use than in 1984. There will be no exact time and date on which library historians will be able to say that libraries were completely automated, although 9:00 a.m. on October 26, 2004 A.D. might appeal to those with a sense of historical neatness.

When automation has had a more significant impact on libraries, and on society in general, what will we be able to say the results have been? A significant aspect of the impact of automation lies in the social climate and the human element. Shaw concluded that, "automation of industry, when achieved on a large scale, will indeed bring with it social and economic changes as drastic as those of the Industrial Revolution."[18] Shera indicated that "of even

greater importance than electronics to the changing pattern
of librarianship is the social milieu in which it will exist."[19]

But it is the human element that is perhaps most important. As Shera put it in a later article, "In this partnership we must not forget that it is the man, not the machine,
who is all-important. The machine does not exist for its
own sake; it does not create its own ends."[20] In the same
vein Dalton has more recently asked, "But ... when there
is a console on the desk of every student who wishes one,
from kindergarten to retired scholar, and when all data systems are compatible, and when every librarian is fully
'aware,' what then is the librarian's role? Is that the end
to be attained? Or just the beginning?"[21]

In "The Library's Role in Society Today," Shaw cited
a question which he liked to ask library administrators:

> Suppose we opened the public treasury to you and
> gave you a steam shovel and trucks to haul the
> money away. Suppose there were no limitation on
> the amount of money you could take except your
> own judgment of what is best for the public you
> serve. Suppose there were no limitations such as
> lack of staff or of suitable staff. Suppose you
> could do this over as many years as were neces-
> sary. Suppose, in a few words, there were no
> excuses and no reasons why you could not supply
> the optimum in library and bibliographical services.
> What would you do?[22]

That question could well be modified, in this context,
to read: Suppose the money is forthcoming and library automation on a large scale becomes a reality not a promise.
What will you do? To ask that question does two things.
It requires us, as we attempt to plan for and use technology,
to examine our approach in terms of what we really wish to
accomplish and not simply in terms of how we can do an
existing routine more expeditiously. It makes us consider
which, of the things we would like to do, we could actually
do now--without the realities of automation--if we put our
minds and energies to it. Obviously we cannot answer that
question with precision but we should nevertheless ask it,
and we can venture a guess as to what part of the answer
might be.

The developments to data in this area have made it

"increasingly evident that successful, large-scale, computer
software systems to handle complex date-access requirements
cannot be developed independently by every large (or small)
library. "[23] Cooperation, long another dream of librarians,
at last seems unavoidable. While libraries are only now establishing guidelines and a firm foundation for a national, regional, and sub-regional library network system, that would
seem to be an essential component of any future development.
One of the major benefits of automation may well be that it
will eventually help to achieve a strong and realistic cooperative sharing of resources by libraries, based on the development and sharing of large-scale, on-line bibliographic
data bases. Immediate knowledge of other libraries' holdings is perhaps the key to effective resource sharing. The
net result should have a significant impact on the personnel,
programs, and services of libraries as well as on the budgets of libraries and their supporting institutions and the allocation of those budgets.

The typical academic library now spends approximately 65 per cent of its budget on personnel, 30 per cent
on resources, and 5 per cent on other costs. Of the 65
per cent devoted to personnel, at least half, and in some
cases three-fifths to two-thirds, is devoted to technical services. The effective implementation of automation should
bring about a reduction in personnel costs, both in technical
services and in public services for housekeeping personnel
(e. g. , file clerks at the circulation desk), accompanied by
an increase in other costs to provide for the development
and maintenance of electronic systems and services. It
should also help further a change in the need for the development of library collections at the local level. That change
in turn should bring about an eventual reduction of acquisitions funds, perhaps a stabilization of those funds, or at
least no need for a significant increase in the percentage of
the library's budget that is given to the support of acquisitions. That is, however, a most sensitive area for, as the
Raffel and Shishko study indicated,[24] both librarians and
users are protective of the acquisitions fund since it is now
viewed as representing the primary purpose of the academic
library. A change in that basic attitude will be necessary
before any substantial reduction or shift of percentage allocation of the acquisitions budget can take place.

A working objective for the internal revision of the
academic library budget might be in the magnitude of providing 60 per cent for personnel, 25-30 per cent for

resources at the local level, and 10-15 per cent for other costs, with a change in the distribution of personnel costs so that the ratio might be one-third for technical services and two-thirds for public services. Eventually the development of automation might help to bring about an institutional reallocation of funds, such as Intrex demanded. The likelihood and extent of such a reallocation is obviously difficult to forecast but, for the larger academic library that now receives 3 per cent of the institution's educational and general budget, a realistic goal might be to seek an increase to 5 per cent. Using an institution with a budget of approximately $66,000,000 and a library budget of approximately $2,000,000 as an example, such reallocations then provide the following budgetary picture.

Present Library Budget
(3% of Institutional Educational and General Budget)

Resources	$ 600,000	(65%)
Personnel	1,300,000	(30%)
Technical Services	650,000	(1/2 of personnel costs)
Public Services	650,000	(1/2 of personnel costs)
Other	100,000	(5%)
Total	$2,000,000	

Present Library Budget Reallocated
(3% of Institutional Educational and General Budget)

Resources	$ 600,000	(30%)
Personnel	1,200,000	(60%)
Technical Services	480,000	(2/5 of personnel)
Public Services	720,000	(3/5 of personnel)
Other	200,000	(10%)
Total	$2,000,000	

Projected Library Budget
(5% of Institutional Educational and General Budget)

Resources	$ 825,000	(25%)
Personnel	1,980,000	(60%)
Technical Services	660,000	(1/3 of personnel)
Public Services	1,320,000	(2/3 of personnel)
Other	495,000	(15%)
Total	$3,300,000	

An examination of those figures, even on a gross basis, indicates the kinds of changes that such reallocations
could bring about. At the local level a substantial increase
in funds would be available for public services personnel,
which has traditionally been the least adequately supported
area in academic libraries. By providing supporting staff
for present professional staff and by expanding the existing
professional staff, academic libraries would no longer be
operating, as they have been, at a minimum service level.
Some have argued as a matter of principle that, "Fundamen-
tally it is only by concentrating all available money on the
purchase of books and manuscript materials that a library
is able to promote scholarship. "[25] It has in the past, however, been more often a matter of priorities, with materials
taking first place. Even within that framework others have
felt that, "Certainly the librarian convinced of the efficacy
of his calling will not cringe at improving or increasing services.... The coordination of faculty services entails little
more than the adaptation of certain special library practices
to an academic institution. "[26]

The essential goal at the local level should be to
bring about an increase in the informational and reference
staff in order to make the library the focal point for infor-
mation-oriented independent study and research within the
college or university. This can and should be supplemented
by direct user access to large-scale bibliographic data bases,
or to augmented catalogs such as Intrex has envisaged, or
to machine guides to the library with perhaps even machine
answering of some basic reference questions. But, to para-
phrase Shaw's conclusion about the future of the book, there
appears to be no probability that any of the mechanical or
electronic devices available or in sight will replace the human being as the means of interrelationship with the type of
materials normally stored and serviced by libraries. Even
beyond the promises of automation there will remain the
book, the librarian, and the reader.

Increased staff at the local level should be used to
provide, among other things: access to machine readable
bibliographic data bases for all users; training and assistance in the use of those data bases; manual searching and
selective dissemination of information to users; stronger
bibliographic support, including verification of bibliographic
references in papers and the provision of abstracts and
translations; substantial improvement in the training of and
assistance to users in those techniques and services;

adequate programs of instruction in the use of the library
and its resources; more complete coverage of library hours
with trained professional staff and more adequate access to
professional reference service for all users; improved access to the library and its services by telephone, campus
mail, video services, etc.; fuller development of local
subject specialists; and the publication of more guides
to collections and services. Consideration should be given
to the ways in which library materials and services can
most effectively be made available to all users in a manner most conducive to the fullest possible support of individual needs without distracting from general needs.
Perhaps automation will enable the library in the academic institution to be relieved of its present conflict as
it tries to decide how, within limited resources, it can
best meet the competing needs of various user groups.

While most of the funds available for other purposes
would be needed to support network maintenance and research
and development, additional funds should also be available to
support the development and implementation of other national,
regional, and sub-regional programs and services. Another
advantage of the broader systems of automation may well be
that the necessity of coming together for these purposes will
help bring about a basic change in attitude that will make
academic institutions and their libraries more willing to sur-
render local autonomy and funds to a central library authority in which they have some controlling voice. A reallocation of funds should foster this new attitude since funds may
be seen as not being taken directly away from the support of
existing programs and services at the local level. But the
development of meaningful and effective programs at these
other levels is also essential. Such programs might include:

1) The establishment, either centrally or in the member libraries, of a strong core of senior subject specialists
whose knowledge and skills would be available to all libraries
and all library users;

2) The effective provision of service staff at the
larger and stronger libraries, to provide access to the collections of those libraries to all users without imposing un-
due costs and strain on the larger and stronger libraries;

3) The implementation of broad and effective programs
of cooperative acquisitions, including the review and evaluation of large and expensive microtext or reprint services,

as well as other expensive potential acquisitions, in terms
of local, regional, and national needs, with a view to making
specific recommendations on the acquisition of such materials
at the appropriate level;

4) The development of collections, either in specific
libraries, or in sub-regional, regional, or national library
centers to make materials more widely and readily available:

5) The operation of a regional lending library and/or
storage facility based on a careful review and analysis of information obtained from a monitoring of use of the central
bibliographic data base;

6) The operation of document and/or user delivery
services designed to maximize access to material by all
users;

7) The implementation of programs such as the North-
east Academic Science Information Center (NASIC), designed
to provide access to a wide variety of specialized machine-
readable bibliographic data bases;

8) The evaluation of commercial machine-based systems so that specific recommendations can be made about
the utilization of such systems either by the network or by
individual libraries;

9) The development of a computer-based library use
monitoring system that would enable libraries effectively to
review and evaluate individual use of the library on a continuing basis and which would provide guaranteed access to
direct personal service where required;

10) The development of equipment and techniques for
providing elementary library orientation, training, and assistance for library users;

11) The establishment of a core of professional and
technical staff to provide effective temporary assistance,
consultative services, and possibly long-term, contracted
library service as well as other kinds of professional assistance and guidance;

12) The implementation of an effective program for the
continuing education of library staff;

13) The implementation of a program and staff designed to assist libraries in undertaking a thorough review of their internal management and operating policies and procedures; and

14) The development and effective implementation of standards for the financial support of libraries and the allocation of that support.

Many of these long-range goals and objectives are not new. They represent programs and services that librarians have discussed for many years but have not yet managed to achieve. The promises of automation should help academic libraries to begin realistically to seek ways of achieving those goals and objectives. If that can be done libraries will be better prepared to plan effectively for large-scale automation and the development of a national library network. Beyond the promises of automation might lie not just the same old, tired library programs and services but new and better programs and services that will enable the library to be a truly effective aid to the user.

Notes

1.   Ralph R. Shaw.   "From Fright to Frankenstein," DC Libraries 24:10, January 1953.

2.   Jesse H. Shera.   "What Is Past Is Prologue: Beyond 1984," ALA Bulletin 61:35, 1967.

3.   Ralph R. Shaw.   "Beyond 1984--A Reply," ALA Bulletin 61:231-2, 1967.

4.   Paul Wasserman.   The Librarian and the Machine. Detroit, Gale, 1965, p. 92.

5.   Ralph R. Shaw.   "Implications for Library Services," Library Quarterly 25:344, 1955

6.   Ibid., pp. 353-4.

7.   Ibid., p. 349.

8.   Shaw.   "Implications for Library Services," op. cit., p. 344.

9.   Carl F. J. Overhage and R. Joyce Harman, eds. In-
     trex; Report of a Planning Conference on Informa-
     tion Transfer Experiments. Cambridge, Mass.,
     The M. I. T. Press, 1965.

10. Paul J. Fasana and Allen Veaner, eds. Collaborative
     Library Systems Development. Cambridge, Mass.,
     The M. I. T. Press, 1971, p. 149.

11. Overhage, op. cit., p. 51.

12. Association of Research Libraries. Academic Library
     Statistics 1964-1965 and Academic Library Statistics
     1973-1974. Washington, D. C., 1965 and 1974.

13. Ellsworth Mason. "Automation, or Russian Roulette?"
     in F. Wilfrid Lancaster, ed. Proceedings of the
     1972 Clinic on Library Applications of Data Process-
     ing: Applications of On-Line Computers to Library
     Problems. Urbana, Illinois, University of Illinois
     Graduate School of Library Science, 1972, p. 139.

14. Ellsworth Mason. Letter, College and Research Li-
     braries 32:316, 1971.

15. Shaw. "Implications for Library Services," op. cit.,
     p. 352.

16. Shera, op. cit., p. 41.

17. Herman H. Fussler. Research Libraries and Tech-
     nology. Chicago, University of Chicago Press,
     1973, p. 9.

18. Shaw. "Implications for Library Services," op. cit.,
     p. 354.

19. Shera, op. cit., p. 42.

20. Jesse H. Shera. "On the Permanence of the Invisible,"
     in his "The Compleat Librarian" and Other Essays.
     Cleveland, The Press of Case Western Reserve,
     1971, p. 18. Originally appeared in his column,
     "Without Reserve," in the Wilson Library Bulletin,
     May 1962.

206   Essays for Ralph Shaw

21. Jack Dalton. "Library Education," in Jerrold Orne, ed. Research Librarianship. New York, Bowker, 1971, pp. 125-6.

22. Ralph R. Shaw. "The Library's Role in Society Today?" in Journal of Education for Librarianship 2:179-80, 1962.

23. Fussler, op. cit., p. 8.

24. Jeffrey A. Raffel and Robert Shishko. Systematic Analysis of University Libraries. Cambridge, Mass., The M.I.T. Press, 1969, pp. 59-60.

25. Eugene B. Barnes. "The University Library--Services or Resources?" Library Quarterly 22:178, 1952.

26. John C. Abbot and David Kaser. "The Coordination of Faculty Services," College and Research Libraries 17:40, 1956.

AFTERWORD

THE APHORISMS OF RALPH SHAW

Ralph Shaw had many interests and was noted for many things. As a dynamic and controversial individual he was a person about whom many anecdotes can be told. Several of those have been mentioned in this volume. To his students he was noted for his pithy, succinct comments which so often aptly summed up a situation or a thought. Having recently been writing biographical sketches of American librarians from earlier in this century, I am keenly aware that most written sources give little idea of the flavor of a person and that once he and his contemporaries are gone, it is difficult to describe what a person was truly like. There are numerous biographical sketches of Ralph Shaw. Several of them, such as the tribute by Lowell Martin in this volume and those by Maurice Tauber, do an excellent job of revealing something of Shaw as a person. Few of them, however, deal adequately with his skill at creating or using aphorisms. As an afterword to our essays, therefore, we have assembled the following list of Shaw aphorisms. It reflects another side of the person and, we hope, will help future biographers more adequately describe him. The list is based on memory and is by no means complete. Nor can we attest that each of the remarks was truly made by Shaw or that it originated with him. Taken as a whole, though, they do reflect the person that he was.

Norman D. Stevens

General

Accept nothing as fact until you have checked it.

Anybody can do anything worse for less.

Every time we don't think a job through and do it right, we think up a new name for it.

Honesty is the best <u>policy</u>.

How I run my library good.

Human effort is worth saving, even if it is your own.

Our basic task, regardless of the kinds of libraries in which we work, deals with books for people.

The shortest distance between two points is around all the angles.

So what?

The social effects of reading upon people who don't read are tremendous.

Why do efficiently something that doesn't need to be done at all?

Administration

Classify jobs, not people.

Each person under you should be smarter and abler than you about what he does.

Good people grow their jobs.

He worries too much about mouse farts.

If it is important and needs doing, there are legal ways of getting it done if you are resourceful.

If the situation is bad enough, anything you do will be an improvement.

If there is a decision to make, you have to make a decision.

If you get a bad building and it's a small one, you can always grow ivy.

It is easier to blame our tools than ourselves.

Our worst mistake when we build a library building is to
keep a dog and do our own barking. Hire a good architect,
give him your program, and leave him alone to work on it.

Parkinson's Law is what happens in the absence of good
personnel administration.

People are the priceless ingredient, not machines.

We often substitute cooperation for thinking through the
whole problem.

[To somebody replacing him while he was on leave]: While
I'm gone you've got to be like horse manure--all over the
place.

Why do we have a dichotomy between what's good for people
and what's good for the library.

Copyright

Anything beyond the copyright notice itself is bullying.

There aren't any good copyright lawyers.

You don't copyright ideas; you copyright a form of presentation of ideas.

Technical Services

The computer has no way of doing things wrong. People
have thousands of ways of doing things wrong.

[Of a computer salesman who presented him with a ridicu-
lously low cost estimate]: He must have had in mind some
kind of horse and sparrow affair.

[Of Ranganathan and library service in India]: The intensity
of interest in classification theory is in direct inverse ratio
to the level of library service.

Machines are useful only when you have a relatively high
frequency of repetitive operations.

[Information scientist]: A man practicing in a field in which
he is not trained and training in a field in which he is not
practicing.

Nothing is impossible. If we can describe it so we can program it, it can be done by machine. The question is
whether it is worth it; what is the trade-off between what
you need to do and what you can do.

[A brief review of Shera's Documentation in Action]: The
publisher put an unnecessary space between in and action.

There is no way for a person to commune with a computer
tape to find things he is not looking for. Giving a person
profiles of stuff he knows he's looking for is only about
50 per cent of the job.

We have installed hardware faster than we have installed
systems for using it.

[A definition of "noise"]: A weed is a flower growing where
you don't want it.

CONTRIBUTORS

For each contributor is listed name, dates of library degrees (and school if other than Rutgers), title of dissertation (and advisor if other than Shaw), and present position.

Susan Artandi. MLS 1959, PhD 1963; Book Indexing by Computer. Professor, Graduate School of Library Service, Rutgers University.

Robert F. Clarke. MLS 1961, PhD 1963; The Impact of Photocopying on Scholarly Publishing. Special Assistant to the Director for Biomedical Communications, U. S. Food and Drug Administration.

Richard M. Dougherty. MLS 1961, PhD 1963; The Scope and Operating Efficiency of Information Centers as Illustrated by the Chemical-Biological Coordination Center of the National Research Council. University Librarian, University of California, Berkeley.

Leonard Grundt. MLS 1960 (Columbia), PhD 1965; An Investigation to Determine the Most Efficient Patterns for Providing Adequate Public Library Service to All Residents of a Typical Large City. Director, Nassau Community College Library, New York.

Ira W. Harris. MLS 1957, PhD 1966; The Influence of Accessibility on Academic Library Use. Professor, Graduate School of Library Studies, University of Hawaii.

Fred J. Heinritz. MLS 1958, PhD 1963; Book Versus Card Catalog Costs. Assistant Director, division of Library Science and Instructional Technology, Southern Connecticut State College.

Peter Hiatt. MLS 1957, PhD 1963; Public Library Branch Services for Adults of Low Education. Dean, School of Librarianship, University of Washington.

Doralyn J. Hickey. MLS 1957, PhD 1962 (Duke University, Religion); Assistant Research Specialist, Graduate School of Library Service, Rutgers University, 1957-1958. Director, School of Library Science, University of Wisconsin-Milwaukee.

Theodore C. Hines. MLS 1958, PhD 1961; The Collectanea as a Bibliographical Tool. Associate Professor, School of Library Service, Columbia University.

Theodore S. Huang. MLS 1961, PhD 1967; Efficacy of Citation Indexing. Director of Libraries, Fairleigh Dickinson University.

Milbrey L. Jones. MLS 1953 (Emory), PhD 1964; Socio-Economic Factors and Library Service to Students (Major Advisor, Mary V. Gaver). Education Program Specialist, Division of Library Programs, U. S. Office of Education.

Choong H. Kim. MLS 1960 (Indiana University), PhD 1964; A Study of Public Library Film Services. Professor, Department of Library Science, Indiana State University.

Norman D. Stevens. MLS 1957, PhD 1961; A Comparative Study of Three Systems of Information Retrieval. Acting Director of University Libraries, University of Connecticut.

Henry Voos. MLS 1953 (Columbia), PhD 1965; Standard Times for Certain Clerical Activities in Technical Processing. Professor, Graduate School of Library Service, Rutgers University.